Cite them right

Palgrave Study Skills

Business Degree Success
Career Skills
Cite Them Right (9th edn)
Critical Thinking Skills (2nd edn)
e-Learning Skills (2nd edn)
The Exam Skills Handbook (2nd edn)
Great Ways to Learn Anatomy and Physiology
The Graduate Career Guidebook
How to Begin Studying English Literature
   (3rd edn)
How to Use Your Reading in Your Essays
   (2nd edn)
How to Write Better Essays (3rd edn)
How to Write Your Undergraduate Dissertation
Improve Your Grammar
Information Skills
The International Student Handbook
The Mature Student's Guide to Writing (3rd edn)
The Mature Student's Handbook
The Palgrave Student Planner
Practical Criticism
Presentation Skills for Students (2nd edn)
The Principles of Writing in Psychology
Professional Writing (3rd edn)
Researching Online
Skills for Success (2nd edn)
The Student Phrase Book
The Student's Guide to Writing (3rd edn)
Study Skills Connected
The Study Skills Handbook (4th edn)
The Study Skills Handbook (Simplified
   Chinese edn)
Study Skills for International Postgraduates
Study Skills for Speakers of English as a
   Second Language
Studying History (3rd edn)
Studying Law (3rd edn)
Studying Modern Drama (2nd edn)
Studying Psychology (2nd edn)

Teaching Study Skills and Supporting Learning
The Undergraduate Research Handbook
The Work-Based Learning Student Handbook
Work Placements – A Survival Guide for Students
Write it Right (2nd edn)
Writing for Engineers (3rd edn)
Writing for Law
Writing for Nursing and Midwifery Students
   (2nd edn)
You2Uni

Pocket Study Skills

14 Days to Exam Success
Blogs, Wikis, Podcasts and More
Brilliant Writing Tips for Students
Completing Your PhD
Doing Research
Getting Critical
Planning Your Dissertation
Planning Your Essay
Planning Your PhD
Reading and Making Notes
Referencing and Understanding Plagiarism
Reflective Writing
Report Writing
Science Study Skills
Studying with Dyslexia
Success in Groupwork
Time Management
Writing for University

Palgrave Research Skills

Authoring a PhD
The Foundations of Research (2nd edn)
Getting to Grips with Doctoral Research
The Good Supervisor (2nd edn)
The Postgraduate Research Handbook
   (2nd edn)
The Professional Doctorate
Structuring Your Research Thesis

For a complete listing of all our titles in this area please visit **www.palgrave.com/studyskills**

Contents

Section H. Modern Humanities Research Association (MHRA) referencing style ... 93

Section I. Oxford University Standard for the Citation of Legal Authorities (OSCOLA) ... 98

Foreword

Welcome to the ninth edition of *Cite them right*. It is hard to believe that it began life in the early 1990s as little more than a single sheet of A4 paper giving guidance on how to reference basic printed sources such as textbooks and journal articles. However, nowadays, the vast range of information available and the rapid developments in electronic publishing and devices mean that continual updating is required.

This book strives to be comprehensive and cover all possible sources for referencing in every academic discipline. We are fortunate that, as practising librarians/information advisers, our constant contact with students and academics allows us to understand more clearly where students struggle with referencing. In many instances, their queries fuel the need to clarify or refine examples and, in some cases, create new ones. We are therefore grateful to our readers for their feedback and reviews on the usefulness of *Cite them right.* We hope that you will continue to provide constructive suggestions in the future.

Principal changes to note from the previous edition

In order to simplify the referencing process, without compromising the ability of readers/tutors to locate the source material, we have made the following important changes to this latest edition:

- Referencing of ebooks, journal and newspaper articles has been simplified by removing unnecessary elements
- The legal material section (including UK statutes) has been expanded to provide fuller Harvard-style examples, and devolved Assemblies legislation has been added
- [Online] is no longer required in references, as it is apparent from the inclusion of the URL
- Titles of online collections/download sites (for example, *Spotify, iTunes* and *Flickr*) have been removed from citation orders and references, as the source is apparent from the URL
- [Downloaded] replaces [Accessed] when you have the source (for example, ebook, music or image) downloaded on an edevice
- In accordance with the publisher's house style, the hyphen in sources such as e-books and e-journals has been omitted, thus ebooks/ejournals.

New material and sources of information

Although this edition represents a complete revision of Harvard and non-Harvard sources, a wide range of new material has been incorporated, namely:

- Non-UK naming conventions
- Books in languages other than English
- Collected works
- Ancient texts
- Unpublished and confidential information
- PowerPoint presentations
- Learning support (study skills) material
- *Facebook*
- Computer games
- Statues, memorials and inscriptions
- Graffiti
- Medical images
- Packaging
- Wills.

How to make the best use of *Cite them right*

Do not be put off by the number of pages in this book – you are *not* expected to read it from cover to cover.

Everyone should read **Sections A–D**, which cover the basics about referencing, quotations and avoiding plagiarism. These will provide you with a much clearer understanding of where you can find the elements that need to be referenced, and the confidence to set them out correctly in your text and reference list.

Section E, the main body of the book, details a comprehensive range of source materials and provides specific examples of how they should be referenced using the Harvard (author-date) referencing style. This system originated in the USA but has become the most widely used referencing style internationally, due to its simplicity and ease of use. However, there is no single authority to define 'Harvard'; hence there are many versions, with slight variations, of the system in use. The alternative title, 'author-date', arises from the fact that the in-text citations follow the format of using the author's surname and the date of publication (where available) to link with the full reference details in the reference list/bibliography.

Use the **Contents** or **Index** pages to identify the type of source you need to reference (for example, ebook, web page, government publication), then follow the advice and example(s) on the relevant page(s).

Sections F–J provide examples for referencing the most commonly used sources in the American Psychological Association (APA), Modern Language Association (MLA), Modern Humanities Research Association (MHRA), Oxford University Standard for Citing of Legal Authorities (OSCOLA) and Vancouver styles.

Each academic institution usually includes recommendations about which referencing style(s) it requires students to use within its academic regulations. If in doubt, you should check with your tutors which style they expect you to use, and ensure you *stick to it consistently*. Likewise, you should ensure that you do not reference using different editions of *Cite them right*, as revisions and updates between editions mean that certain guidelines and examples have changed (see previous section). Use one edition only. If your tutor does not stipulate a specific edition, make it clear to them which edition you are using.

From the outset, our aim was always to produce a guide that was manageable and easy to follow for everyone, rather than a hefty tome that would intimidate students. Please note that the layout of the text and example boxes throughout, that is, in columns and including varying amounts of white space, is deliberate. The aim is to increase clarity, and facilitate easier reading and note-making. It should also be of assistance to those students with specific learning difficulties. Although we initially considered providing more than one example for each source, we felt that this would prove detrimental, believing that one boxed example acts as a clear template for the student's own citations/references.

A **Glossary** is included to explain the meaning of certain terms used in the text. These words appear in bold when they first occur within each section.

Richard Pears and Graham Shields, 2013

Acknowledgements

The authors would like to thank:

The House of Commons Information Office for permission to quote from *Factsheet G17: The Official Report*

Colleagues at Durham University and the University of Cumbria for their advice, and in particular Mamtimyn Sunuodula, Area Studies librarian, Durham University Library

Staff and students at other academic institutions for their support, constructive feedback and suggestions

Section A.
What is referencing and why is it important?

What is referencing?

Fundamentally, referencing is the process of acknowledging the sources you have used in writing your essay, assignment or piece of work. It allows the reader to access your source documents as quickly and easily as possible in order to verify, if necessary, the validity of your arguments and the evidence on which they are based. You identify these sources by citing them in the text of your assignment (called **citations** or **in-text citations**) and referencing them at the end of your assignment (called the **reference list** or **end-text citations**). The reference list only includes the sources cited in your text. It is not the same thing as a **bibliography**, which uses the same referencing style, but also includes all material, for example background readings, used in the preparation of your work.

To reference successfully, it is essential that, as a matter of course, you systematically save full details, for example author, date, title, publication details, **URL**, of any material you use *at the time you use it*. Besides being good academic practice, this ensures that you do not have the problem of trying to find sources you may have used weeks or months previously.

By referring to the works of established authorities and experts in your subject area, you can add weight to your comments and arguments. This helps to demonstrate that you have read widely, and considered and analysed the writings of others. Remember, good referencing can help you attain a better grade or mark (often between five and ten per cent of the total). Most importantly, good referencing is essential to avoid any possible accusation of **plagiarism** (see section below).

There are electronic bibliographic tools available that will store and manage your references while you are writing your assignment. Most academic institutions subscribe to some kind of referencing software packages such as *Refworks* or *Endnote*. *Refworks* is more often used by undergraduates and taught postgraduates, while *Endnote* contains more advanced features of particular benefit to researchers and authors. It is worth pointing out that, if you use any of these tools, you will still need to double-check your citations and references to ensure that they are consistent and compatible with your institution's/tutor's guidelines.

What is plagiarism?

Plagiarism is a term that describes the unacknowledged use of someone's work. This includes material or ideas from any (published or unpublished) sources, whether print, web-based (even if freely available) or audiovisual. Using the words or ideas of others without referencing your source would be construed as plagiarism and is a very serious academic offence. At the end of the day, it is regarded as stealing intellectual property.

The following are considered forms of plagiarism:
- Passing off as your own a piece of work that is partly or wholly the work of another student

- Citing and referencing sources that you have not used
- **Quoting**, **summarising** or **paraphrasing** material in your assignment without citing the original source (see Section C)
- 'Recycling' a piece of your own work that you have previously submitted for another module or course (ie self-plagiarism).

How can you avoid plagiarism?

In many cases, students who find themselves accused of plagiarising often have done so unintentionally. Poor organisation and time management, as well as a failure to understand good academic practice, are often to blame. You might therefore find it helpful to note the following points:

- Manage your time and plan your work – ensure that you have enough time to prepare, read and write
- When paraphrasing an author's text, ensure that you use your own words, sentence structure and writing style (see Section C)
- In your notes, highlight in colour/bold any **direct quotations** you want to use in your assignment – this will help to ensure that you use quotation marks with an appropriate reference when you are writing up your work
- Allow enough time to check your final draft for possible referencing errors or omissions: for example, check that all your in-text citations have a corresponding entry in your reference list, and vice versa

- Save all your notes, files, printouts and so on until you receive your final mark or grade.

What is common knowledge?

In all academic or professional fields, experts regard some ideas as **common knowledge**. This is generally defined as facts, dates, events and information that are expected to be known by someone studying or working in a particular field. The facts can be found in numerous places and are likely to be known by many people: for example, that Margaret Thatcher was a British prime minister. Such information does not generally have to be referenced. However, as a student, you may have only just started to study a particular subject, so the material you are reading may not yet be common knowledge to you. In order to decide if the material you want to use in your assignment constitutes common knowledge, you need to ask yourself the following questions:

- Did I know this information before I started my course?
- Did this information/idea come from my own brain?

If the answer to either or both of the questions is 'no', then the information is not common knowledge to you. In these cases you need to cite and reference your source(s).

What about confidential information?

In a number of subject areas you may need to use source material that is confidential, for example medical or legal material. This information, by its nature, is unpublished and not in the public domain. Usually, your tutor will offer guidance on whether you can use the information and reference it. In some cases, it will be possible to anonymise the documents, allowing you to refer to them for argument or statistical purposes, for example 'Patient X' or 'Placement hospital'. In other cases, you may be able to obtain permission from all those who might be affected by its publication. If in any doubt, you should consult the person or organisation that produced the information for permission to use it. See Section 5.5 for details on how to reference confidential information.

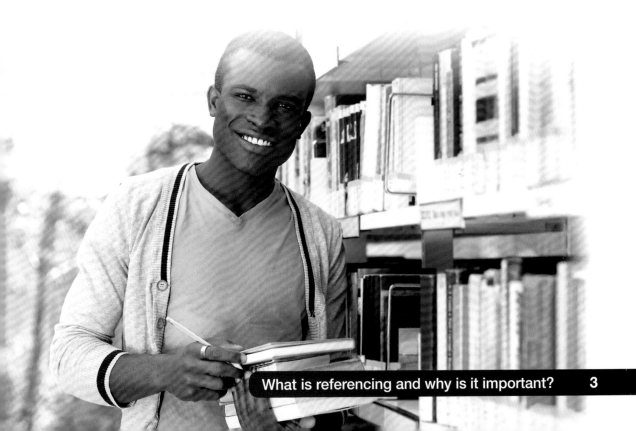

Section B.
Setting out citations in your text

Setting out citations

It is important to remember that **citations** in your assignments must be included in the final word count.

In-text citations give the brief (abbreviated) details of the work that you are quoting from, or to which you are referring in your text. These citations will then link to the full **reference** in your **reference list** at the end of your work, which is arranged in alphabetical order by author. Works cited in appendices, but not in the main body of your text, should still be included in your reference list. It is important to note that **footnotes** and **endnotes** are not used in Harvard and other author-date referencing styles.

There are several ways in which you can incorporate citations into your text, depending on your own style and the flow of the work. However, a tutor or supervisor may advise you on their preferred format. You can see from the examples below how you can vary the use of citations in your text.

Your citations should include the following elements:

- Author(s) or editor(s) surname/family name
  NB For non-UK names, see Section D
- Year of publication
- Page number(s) if required (always required for lengthy or **direct quotations**).

If you are quoting directly or using ideas from a specific page or pages of a work, you should include the page number(s) in your citations. Insert the abbreviation p. (or pp.) before the page number(s).

> **Example**
>
> Harris (2008, p. 56) argued that 'nursing staff …'

If your citation refers to a complete work or to ideas that run through an entire work, your citation would simply use the author and date details.

> **Example**
>
> In a recent study (Evans, 2010), qualifications of school-leavers were analysed …

Citing one author/editor

Cite the author/editor.

> **Example**
>
> In his autobiography (Fry, 2010) …

Citing a corporate author

Cite the name (or initials, if well known) of the corporate body.

> **Examples**
>
> … as shown in its annual report (BBC, 2012).
>
> … the popularity of visiting historical monuments (English Heritage, 2011).

Citing two authors/editors

Both are listed.

> **Example**
>
> Recent educational research (Lewis and Jones, 2012) …

Citing three authors/editors

All three are listed.

> **Example**
>
> In an important study of the subject (Hill, Smith and Reid, 2010) …

Citing four or more authors/editors

Cite the first name listed in the source followed by **et al.** (meaning 'and others').

> **Example**
>
> New research on health awareness by Tipton *et al*. (2012) …

NB All authors'/editors' names would be given in your reference list (no matter how many there are) so that each author or editor can receive credit for their research and published work.

Citing a source with no author/editor

Where the name of an author/editor cannot be found, use the title (in italics). Do not use 'Anon' or 'Anonymous'.

> **Example**
>
> In a groundbreaking survey (*Health of the nation*, 2011) …

Citing multiple sources

If you need to refer to two or more publications at the same time, these can be listed separated by semicolons (;). The publications should be cited in chronological order (with the earliest date first). If more than one work is published in the same year, then they should be listed alphabetically by author/editor.

> **Example**
>
> A number of environmental studies (Town, 2009; Williams, 2010; Andrews *et al*., 2011; Martin and Richards, 2013) considered …

Citing sources published in the same year by the same author

Sometimes you may need to cite two (or more) publications by an author published in the same year. To distinguish between the items in the text, allocate lower case letters in alphabetical order after the publication date.

> **Example**
>
> In his study of the work of Rubens, Miller (2006a) emphasised the painter's mastery of drama. However, his final analysis on this subject (Miller, 2006b) argued that …

In your reference list, the publications would look like this.

> **Example**
>
> Miller, S. (2006a) *The Flemish masters*. London: Phaidon Press.
>
> Miller, S. (2006b) *Rubens and his art*. London: Killington Press.

Citing different editions of the same work by the same author

Separate the dates of publication with a semicolon (;) with the earliest date first.

> **Example**
>
> In both editions (Hawksworth, 2009; 2013) …

Citing sources with multiple authors

If you want to cite a book edited by Holmes and Baker, which has, for example, ten contributors and does not specify who wrote each section or chapter, follow the format of citing using the editors' names.

> **Example**
>
> Recent research (Holmes and Baker, 2009, pp. 411–428) proved …

NB See Section E1.9 (Chapters/sections of edited books) for the relevant information on citing and referencing when the author's name is given for a specific chapter or section.

Citing a source with no date

Use the phrase 'no date'.

> **Example**
>
> In an interesting survey of youth participation in sport, the authors (Harvey and Williams, no date) …

Citing a source with no author or date

Use the title and 'no date'.

> **Example**
>
> Integrated transport systems clearly work (*Trends in European transport systems*, no date).

Citing a web page

If you are citing a **web page**, it should follow the preceding guidelines, citing by: author and date where possible; by title and date if there is no identifiable author; or, as shown below, by **URL** if neither author nor title can be identified.

> **Example**
>
> The latest survey of health professionals (http://www.onlinehealthsurvey.org, 2012) reveals that …

For more details on how to cite and reference web pages, see Section E8 (The internet).

Secondary referencing: citing/referencing a work that has been cited in another source

In some cases you will want to cite/reference a work mentioned or quoted in another author's work. This is known as **secondary referencing**, as you have not actually seen this original source yourself. If you can, you should try to locate and verify the details of the source referred to. If you can locate it, then you can reference it as normal.

In the text of your essay or assignment, you should cite both sources and use the phrase 'quoted in' or 'cited in', depending on whether the author of the work you are reading is directly quoting or summarising from the original.

> ### Examples
>
> Harvey (2010, quoted in Lewis, 2012, p. 43) provides an excellent survey …
>
> White's views on genetic abnormalities in crops (2011, cited in Murray, 2012) support the idea that …

If you were unable to read Harvey's or White's works yourself, you cannot include them in your reference list. They would only appear as citations, as in the examples above.

Section C.
Quoting, paraphrasing and summarising in your text

Setting out quotations

Quotations should be relevant to your arguments and used judiciously in your text. Excessive use of quotations can disrupt the flow of your writing and prevent you from demonstrating your understanding and analysis of the sources you have read. Your tutor will prefer to read your own interpretation of the evidence.

Bear in mind that **direct quotations** are also counted in your assignment's total word count.

Short direct quotations (up to two or three lines) should be enclosed in quotation marks (single or double – be consistent) and included in the body of your text. Give the author, date and page number(s)/URL that the quotation was taken from.

> **Example**
>
> 'If you need to illustrate the idea of nineteenth-century America as a land of opportunity, you could hardly improve on the life of Albert Michelson' (Bryson, 2004, p. 156).

Longer quotations should be entered as a separate paragraph and indented from the main text. Quotation marks are not required.

> **Example**
>
> King (1997) describes the intertwining of fate and memory in many evocative passages, such as:
>
> > So the three of them rode towards their end of the Great Road, while summer lay all about them, breathless as a gasp. Roland looked up and saw something that made him forget all about the Wizard's Rainbow. It was his mother, leaning out of her apartment's bedroom window: the oval of her face surrounded by the timeless gray stone of the castle's west wing. (King, 1997, pp. 553–554)

Making changes to quotations

Omitting part of a quotation

Indicate this by using three dots … (called **ellipsis**).

> **Example**
>
> 'Drug prevention … efforts backed this up' (Gardner, 2007, p. 49).

Inserting your own, or different, words into a quotation

Put them in square brackets [ ].

> **Example**
>
> 'In this field [crime prevention], community support officers …' (Higgins, 2008, p. 17).

Pointing out an error in a quotation

Do not correct the error; instead write [*sic*].

> ### Example
>
> Williams (2008, p. 86) noted that 'builders maid [*sic*] bricks'.

Retaining/modernising historical spellings

Decide to either retain the original spelling, or modernise the spelling and note this in your text.

> ### Examples
>
> 'Hast thou not removed one Grain of Dirt and Rhubbish?' (Kent, 1727, p. 2).
>
> 'Have you not removed one grain of dirt or rubbish?' (Kent, 1727, p. 2, spelling modernised).

Emphasising part of a quotation

Put the words you want to emphasise in italics and state that you have added the emphasis.

> ### Example
>
> 'Large numbers of *women* are more prepared to support eco-friendly projects' (Denby, 2006, p. 78, my italics).

If the original text uses italics, state that the italics are in the original source.

> ### Example
>
> 'The dictionary is based on *rigorous analysis* of the grammar of the language' (Soanes, 2004, p. 2, italics in original).

Paraphrasing

When you **paraphrase**, you express someone else's writing in your own words, usually to achieve greater clarity. This is an alternative way of referring to an author's ideas or arguments without using direct quotations from their text. Used properly, it has the added benefit of fitting more neatly into your own style of writing and allows you to demonstrate that you really do understand what the author is saying. However, you must ensure that you do not change the original meaning and you must still cite and reference your source of information.

> ### Example
>
> Harrison (2007, p. 48) clearly distinguishes between the historical growth of the larger European nation states and the roots of their languages and linguistic development, particularly during the fifteenth and sixteenth centuries. At this time, imperial goals and outward expansion were paramount for many of the countries, and the effects of spending on these activities often led to internal conflict.

Summarising

When you **summarise**, you provide a brief statement of the main points of an article, **web page**, chapter or book, known as a summary. This differs from paraphrasing as it only lists the main topics or headings, with most of the detailed information being left out.

Example

Nevertheless, one important study (Harrison, 2007) looks closely at the historical and linguistic links between European races and cultures over the past five hundred years.

Section D.
Creating references in your reference list/bibliography

Points to note

Students often find it difficult to differentiate between the terms **reference list** and **bibliography**.

The reference list is the detailed list of **references** cited in your assignment. It includes the full bibliographical information on sources, so that the reader can identify and locate the work/item.

A bibliography also provides a detailed list of references but includes background readings or other material you may have consulted, but not cited, in your text.

You should always check with your tutors whether they require you to include a reference list, a bibliography, or both (where you would provide a reference list and a separate bibliography of background readings). Either way, both are located at the end of your essay/piece of work. In the Harvard system, they are always arranged in alphabetical order by the author's surname/family name or, when there is no author, by title. For **web pages** where no author or title is apparent, the **URL** address should be used.

The fundamental points are that the reference links with your **citation** and includes enough information for the reader to be able to readily find the source again.

Example

In-text citation

In a recently published survey (Hill, Smith and Reid, 2010, p. 93), the authors argue that …

Reference list

Hill, P., Smith, R. and Reid, L. (2010) *Education in the 21st century*. London: Educational Research Press.

It is important that in your references you follow the format exactly for all sources, as shown in each example in Section E. This includes following the instructions consistently regarding the use of capital letters, typeface and punctuation.

Non-UK naming conventions

Across the world there are several practices for naming individual people, including given name followed by family name (for example John Smith), family name followed by given name (for example Smith John), given name alone (for example John) and given name followed by father's name (for example John son of James). Within one country there may be several naming conventions employed by different ethnic groups.

When referencing names of authors in your work, you may be required to use a preferred naming convention. If in doubt, ask for advice from tutors or publishers, or copy the authors' expressions of their names. The principle followed in *Cite them right* (as with other authorities) is to place the family name first in the citation, followed by the initials of given names. The following examples show the complexity of this issue.

Arabic names

The given name precedes the family name. For example, Najīb Maḥfūz would be referenced as:

> **Example**
>
> Maḥfūz, N. (1980) *Afrāḥ al-qubbah* (Wedding song). al-Fajjālah: Maktabat Miṣr.

Yusuf al-Qaradawi would be referenced as:

> **Example**
>
> Qaradawi, Y. (2003) *The lawful and the prohibited in Islam*. London: Al-Birr Foundation.

Tariq Ramadan would be referenced as:

> **Example**
>
> Ramadan, T. (2008) *Radical reform: Islamic ethics and liberation*. Oxford: Oxford University Press.

When a man has completed the Hajj pilgrimage to Mecca, he may include Hajji in his name, for example Ragayah Hajji Mat Zin. Follow the order for the person's name given in the publication. For example, Ragayah Hajji Mat Zin would be referenced as:

> **Example**
>
> Ragayah, H.M.Z. (2008) *Corporate governance: role of independent non-executive directors*. Bangi: Institut Kajian Malaysia dan Antarabangsa, Universiti Kebangsaan Malaysia.

Burmese names

Individuals are usually referenced by the first element of their name. For example, Aung San Suu Kyi would be referenced as:

> **Example**
>
> Aung, S.S.K. (1991) *Freedom from fear and other writings*. London: Viking.

Chinese names

Traditionally, the family name is the first element of the individual's name and when citing use this first, as with Western names. For example, Hu Sen appears as Sen Hu in Western convention on the book title page, but in Chinese tradition would be referenced as:

> **Example**
>
> Hu, S. (2001) *Lecture notes on Chern-Simons-Witten theory*. Singapore and River Edge, New Jersey: World Scientific.

Zhang Boshu would be referenced as:

> **Example**
>
> Zhang, B. (1994) *Marxism and human sociobiology: the perspective of economic reforms in China*. Albany, NY: State University of New York Press.

If the author has adopted the convention of placing family name last, invert the elements as with Western names. For example, Sophia Tang would be referenced as:

> ### Example
>
> Tang, S. (2009) *Electronic consumer contracts in the conflict of laws*. Oxford: Hart Publishing.

Indian names

The given name precedes the family name. For example, Mohandas Gandhi would be referenced as:

> ### Example
>
> Gandhi, M.K. (1927) *An autobiography, or, the story of my experiments with truth*. Translated from the original in Gujarati by Mahadev Desa. Ahmedabad: Navajivan Press.

Japanese names

The family name precedes the given name. For example, Ōe Kenzaburō would be referenced as:

> ### Example
>
> Ōe, K. (1994) *The pinch runner memorandum*. Armonk, NY: M.E. Sharpe.

Note that many Japanese authors are known by given name then family name, for example Kenzaburō Ōe.

Malaysian names

Malay names may have a given name followed by a patronym or father's name, for example Nik Safiah Nik Ismail. Some names may have the family name followed by given names:

> ### Example
>
> Nik, S.N.I. (2010) *Soft skills: the what, the why, the how*. Bangi: Penerbit Universiti Kebangsaan Malaysia.

Portuguese names

In Portuguese naming conventions, individuals have a given name followed by their mother's family name and then their father's family name. Reference the father's family name first. For example, Armando Gonçalves Pereira would be referenced as:

> ### Example
>
> Pereira, A.G. (1949) *Algumas lições, conferências e discursos*. Lisbon: Editorial Império.

For names with particles, reference this after the initials of the given names. For example, André Luiz de Souza Filgueira would be referenced as:

> ### Example
>
> Souza Filgueira, A.L. de (2012) 'A utopia nacionalista de Manoel Bomfim', *Em Tempo de Histórias*, 20, pp. 153–163.

Spanish names

Traditionally, Spanish/Latin American individuals have a given name followed by their father's family name and then their mother's family name. When referencing these compound names, use the father's family name, following conventions for Western, Arabic and many other naming styles. For example, Pedro Vallina Martínez would be referenced as:

Example

Vallina Martínez, P. (1968) *Mis memorias*. México & Caracas: Tierra y Libertad.

Thai names

The given name is followed by the family name. For example, Piti Disyatat would be referenced as:

Example

Disyatat, P. (2011) 'The bank lending channel revisited', *Journal of Money, Credit and Banking*, 43(4), pp. 711–734.

Vietnamese names

Individuals are referenced by their family name, the first element of their names. For example, Võ Nguyên Giáp would be referenced as:

Example

Võ, N.G. (1975) *Unforgettable days*. Hanoi: Foreign Languages Publishing House.

Names with particles/prefixes

These are names that include, for example, d', de, de los, le, van and von.

It is difficult to provide definitive examples for all names with particles/prefixes, as each language has its own rules. As mentioned above, where possible copy the authors' own expressions of their names from the publication you are viewing and, if in any doubt, use the **internet** or library catalogues to confirm the details.

Elements that you may need to include in your references

Generally, the elements for inclusion for any source should be self-evident. Use the 'citation order' listed with the examples in Section E to help you identify the elements you should be looking for. Below, guidance is provided on where to look for these elements when referencing some of the most commonly used sources:

- *For books:* look on the title page or back of the title page (verso)
- *For printed journal articles:* look at the beginning of the article or at the table of contents of the journal issue
- *For electronic journal articles:* look at the top of the first page (before or after the article title)
- *For web pages:* look at the top and bottom of the first page, the logos and, for the URL, in the **address bar** at the top of your screen. You may find it helpful to right-click on the mouse and select 'Properties': this will often display the date the web page was last updated/ modified.

Authors/editors

- Include all contributing names in the order they appear, for example Hill, P., Smith, R. and Reid, L.
- Put the surname/family name first, followed by the initial(s) of given names, for example Hill, P.
  NB For non-UK names, see section above

- Some publications are written/produced by corporate bodies or organisations and you can use this name as the author, for example the National Trust. Note that the corporate author may also be the publisher
- If the publication is compiled by an editor or editors, signify this by using the abbreviation (ed.) or (eds), for example Parker, G. and Rouxeville, A. (eds)
- Do not use 'Anon' if the author/editor is anonymous or no author/editor can be identified. Use the title of the work.

Year/date of publication

- Give the year of publication in round brackets after the author's/editor's name, for example Smith, L. (2012)
- If no date of publication can be identified, use (no date), for example Smith, L. (no date).

Title

- Use the title as given, together with the subtitle (if any), for example *Studying and working in Spain: a student guide*.

Edition

- Only include the edition if it is not the first edition or if it is a revised edition (without a number, see below).
- Edition is abbreviated to edn (to avoid confusion with the abbreviation ed. or eds for editor or editors), for example 3rd edn or Rev. edn.

Place of publication and publisher

- Only required for printed books, reports etc.
- Separate the place of publication and the publisher with a colon, for example London: Initial Music Publishing
- If there is more than one place of publication listed for the publisher, reference the first or most prominent
- For places of publication in the USA, add the abbreviated US state name (unless otherwise obvious), for example Cambridge, Mass.: Harvard University Press
- If a source is unpublished, please refer to Section E5.

Series/volumes (for books)

- Include series and individual volume number, if relevant, after the publisher, for example Oxford: Clio Press (World Bibliographical Series, 60).

Issue information (for journals and newspapers)

- When provided, you need to include the following information in the order:
  – volume number
  – issue/part number
  – date or season
  for example 87(3); or 19 July; or summer.

Page numbers

- Page numbers are only required in the reference list for chapters in books, and journal/newspaper articles
- The abbreviation p. is used for single pages and pp. for more than one, for example London: River Press, pp. 90–99.

ISBNs

- Although ISBNs (International Standard Book Numbers) represent unique identifiers for books and eliminate confusion about editions and reprints, they are not commonly used in references.

URLs (Uniform/Universal Resource Locators)

- When using the URL address for web pages, you can shorten it, as long as the route remains clear
- Include the date you accessed the web page, for example (Accessed: 14 Feb 2012), or downloaded an ebook/music (Downloaded: 14 June 2013).

Digital Object Identifiers (dois)

- **Digital Object Identifiers** (dois) tag individual digital (online) sources. These sources can range from journal articles to conference papers and presentations. They include a number identifying the publisher, work and issue information. The following example shows how the doi replaces the URL in the reference; note that, as the doi is the permanent identifier for the source, it is not necessary to include an accessed date.

> ### Example
>
> Horch, E.P. and Zhou, J. (2012) 'Charge-coupled device speckle observations of binary stars', *Astronomical Journal*, 136, pp. 312–322. doi: 10.1088/0004-6256/136/1/312.

- You or your reader can locate a source by entering its doi in an internet search engine.

Journal articles using article numbers and dois

- Some publishers now use article numbers instead of issue and page numbers
- The reference to the article includes the number of pages in the article
- Note that to see the page numbers, you may need to open the pdf version of the article. If this is not available, you may need to refer to the section number or even number the paragraphs and cite one of these for your reference, for example section 2.2, paragraph 3.

Example

Bond, J.W. (2008) 'On the electrical characteristics of latent finger mark corrosion of brass', *J. Phys. D: Appl. Phys*, 41, 125502 (10pp). doi: 10.1088/0022-3727/41/12/125502.

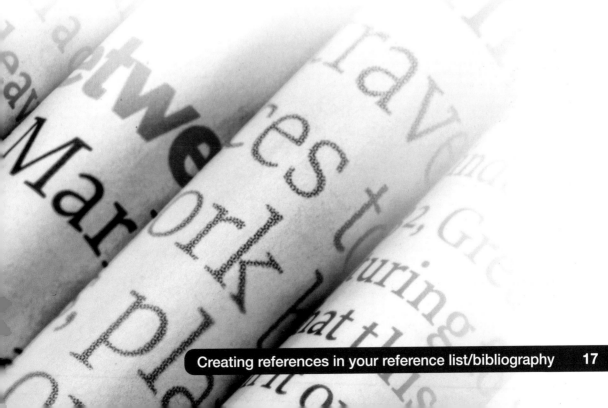

Sample text and reference list using Harvard (author-date) referencing style

NB This text makes extensive use of references for illustrative purposes only.

Text

A comparative study conducted by Bowman and Jenkins (2011), on properties built within the last twenty years and older houses, clearly illustrated the financial and environmental benefits of investing time and money in improving home insulation. A recent survey (Thermascan, 2012) and video (Norman, 2012) underlined that as much as a third of the heat generated in homes is lost through the walls or the roof as a result of poor insulation.

An article by Hallwood (2012) was fulsome in its praise of the work of organisations such as Tadea and the Energy Saving Trust in producing public information packs providing guidance on cavity wall and loft insulation. Further studies show that the amount of energy needed to heat our homes can have an ever-increasing impact on both the environment and family finances (BBC, 2010; Department of the Environment, 2011; Hampson and Carr, 2011). However, there is some criticism in the literature of the conflicting information regarding installation costs and the subsequent savings to be made (Kirkwood, Harper and Jones, 2011, pp. 49–58).

The relationship between climate change and energy use has been clearly emphasised by energy companies aiming to help potential customers 'supply their own energy with technologies such as solar panels and ground source heat pumps' (British Gas, 2012, p. 8). But huge challenges are posed by the conflict between expensive sustainable energy and family economic constraints, and these issues are examined in detail by Young (2012). What remains clear is that by finding ways in which we can significantly reduce our home running costs, we can simultaneously substantially reduce our carbon footprint (Strathearn, 2013).

Reference list

NB This list incorporates bubble captions to identify the type of source being referenced, which are used for illustrative purposes only.

BBC (2010) *Energy use and the environment*. Available at http://www.bbc.co.uk/energy (Accessed: 18 August 2012).

web page — see Section E8

Bowman, R. and Jenkins, S. (2011) 'Financial and environmental issues and comparisons in new and old build properties', in Harris, P. (ed.) *Studies on property improvements and environmental concerns in modern Britain*. London: Pinbury, pp. 124–145.

chapter in edited book

see Section E1.9

British Gas (2012) *A green light to save you more*. Eastbourne: British Gas.

company pamphlet/booklet

see Section E1.18

Department of the Environment (2011) *Energy and the environment in Britain today*. Available at: http://www.doe.gov.uk (Accessed: 12 January 2013).

online government report

see Section E13.2

Hallwood, L. (2012) 'The good work of sustainable energy organisations continues', *The Times*, 20 June, pp. 20–21.

electronic or print newspaper article

see Section E3

Hampson, P. and Carr, L. (2011) 'The impact of rising energy use on the environment: a five-year study', *Journal of Energy and Environmental Issues*, 53(5), pp. 214–231.

electronic or print journal article

see Section E2

Kirkwood, L., Harper, S. and Jones, T. (2011) *The DIY culture in Britain: costs for homes and the nation*. Available at: http://www.amazon.co.uk/kindle-ebooks (Downloaded: 8 September 2012).

signifies held on your own device

ebook downloaded onto edevice

see Section E1.2

Norman, L. (2012) *Heat loss in houses*. Available at http://www.youtube.com/watchheatlosshouseclm (Accessed: 18 March 2013).

YouTube video — see Section E20.9F

Strathearn, G. (2013) *Energy and environmental issues for the 21st century*. Basingstoke: Palgrave Macmillan.

print or electronic book

see Section E1

Thermascan (2012) *A report into costs and benefits relating to heat loss in homes*. Birmingham: Thermascan.

printed report — see Section E11

Young, L. (2012) *Sustaining our energy: challenges and conflicts*. Available at: http://books.google.com (Downloaded: 12 November 2012).

signifies held on your own device

ebook downloaded onto edevice

see Section E1.2

Checklist of what to include in your reference list for the most common information sources

	Author	Year of publication	Title of article/chapter	Title of publication	Issue information (volume/part numbers if available)	Place of publication	Publisher	Edition	Page number(s)	URL/doi	Date accessed/downloaded
Book	✓	✓		✓		✓	✓	✓			
Chapter from book	✓	✓	✓	✓		✓	✓	✓	✓		
Ebook	✓	✓		✓						URL if required	✓
Journal article (print and electronic)	✓	✓	✓	✓	✓				✓	doi if required	
Web page	✓	✓		✓						✓	✓
Newspaper article (print and electronic)	✓	✓	✓	✓	✓				✓		

Top 10 tips

1. Be aware: if you don't already know, check with your tutor which referencing style you are expected to use
2. Be positive: used properly, references strengthen your writing, demonstrating that you have spent time researching and digesting material and produced your own opinions and arguments
3. Be decisive about the best way to cite your sources and how you balance your use of direct quotations, paraphrasing and summarising (read about these in the introductory sections of *Cite them right*)
4. Be willing to ask for help: library/ learning resource staff offer support with referencing and academic skills
5. Be organised: prepare well and keep a record of all potentially useful sources as you find them
6. Be prepared: read the introductory sections of *Cite them right* before you begin your first assignment
7. Be consistent: once you have established the referencing style required, use it consistently throughout your piece of work
8. Be patient: make time and take your time to ensure that your referencing is accurate
9. Be clear: clarify the type of source you are referencing and check *Cite them right* for examples
10. Be thorough: check through your work and your references before you submit your assignment, ensuring that your citations all match with a full reference and vice versa.

Section E.
Examples of sources using the Harvard style

NB Before looking at specific examples in this section, you should ensure that you have read Sections B, C and D.

1. Books, including ebooks

In previous editions of *Cite them right*, distinctions were made between print and electronic versions of sources. The increasing availability of ebooks in identical form to print has rendered this distinction between versions unnecessary. If the online source includes all the elements seen in print versions (ie publication details, edition and page numbers), reference in the same way as print.

1.1 Printed books

Citation order:
- Author/editor
- Year of publication (in round brackets)
- Title (in italics)
- Edition (only include the edition number if it is not the first edition)
- Place of publication: publisher
- Series and volume number (where relevant)

Example: book with one author

In-text citation

According to Bell (2010, p. 23), the most important part of the research process is …

Reference list

Bell, J. (2010) *Doing your research project*. 5th edn. Maidenhead: Open University Press.

Example: book with two or three authors

In-text citation

Goddard and Barrett (2007) suggested …

Reference list

Goddard, J. and Barrett, S. (2007) *The health needs of young people leaving care*. Norwich: University of East Anglia, School of Social Work and Psychosocial Studies.

Example: book with more than three authors

In-text citation

This was proved by Young *et al.* (2005) …

Reference list

Young, H.D., Freedman, R.A., Sandin, T. and Ford, A. (2005) *Sears and Zemansky's university physics*. 10th edn. San Francisco: Addison-Wesley.

Example: book with an editor

In-text citation

The formation of professions was examined in Prest (1987).

Reference list

Prest, W. (ed.) (1987) *The professions in early modern England*. London: Croom Helm.

Example: book with author(s) and editor(s)

In-text citation

Caroline (2007) points out …

Reference list

Caroline, N.L. (2007) *Nancy Caroline's emergency care in the streets*. 6th edn. Edited by Andrew N. Pollak, Bob Fellows and Mark Woolcock. Sudbury, Mass.: Jones and Bartlett.

Example: book with no author

In-text citation

The Percy tomb has been described as 'one of the master-pieces of medieval European art' (*Treasures of Britain*, 1990, p. 84).

Reference list

Treasures of Britain and treasures of Ireland (1990) London: Reader's Digest Association Ltd.

1.2   Ebooks

When an ebook looks like a printed book, with publication details and pagination, you should reference as a printed book (see Section 1.1 above).

Citation order:

- Author/editor
- Year of publication (in round brackets)
- Title of book (in italics)
- Place of publication: publisher

Example

In-text citation

In their analysis, Hremiak and Hudson (2011, pp. 36–39) …

Reference list

Hremiak, A. and Hudson, T. (2011) *Understanding learning and teaching in secondary schools*. Harlow: Pearson Longman.

On some *personal edevices* (Kobo, Kindle/Kindle Fire, Sony, smartphones and tablets), specific ebook pagination details are often not available, so use the information you do have (loc, %, chapter/page), for example (Richards, 2012, 67%); (Winters, 2011, ch. 4, p. 12).

When downloading ebooks, you may find it helpful to add a general statement at the end of your reference list informing your tutor that the texts are available on your edevice. You should also include the date that you downloaded them.

Citation order:
- Author/editor
- Year of publication (in round brackets)
- Title of book (in italics)
- Available at: URL
- (Downloaded: date)

Example

In-text citation

Arthur's argument with the council was interrupted by the Vogon Constructor Fleet (Adams, 1979, loc 876).

Reference list

Adams, D. (1979) *The hitchhiker's guide to the galaxy*. Available at: http://www.amazon.co.uk/kindle-ebooks (Downloaded: 29 January 2013).

1.3   Audiobooks

Citation order:
- Author/editor
- Year of publication/release (in round brackets)
- Title of book (in italics)
- Narrated by (if required)
- Available at: URL
- (Downloaded: date)

Example

In-text citation

Covering 2000 years of medical history, Cunningham (2007) …

Reference list

Cunningham, A. (2007) *The making of modern medicine*. Available at: http://www.audiogo.com/uk/ (Downloaded: 18 March 2013).

1.4   Reprint editions

For reprints of old books, usually only the year of the original publication (not the publisher) is given, along with the full publication facts of the reprint.

Citation order:
- Author/editor
- Year of original publication (in round brackets)
- Title of book (in italics)
- Reprint
- Place of reprint publication: reprint publisher
- Year of reprint

Example

In-text citation

One of the first critics of obfuscation (David, 1968) …

Reference list

David, M. (1968) *Towards honesty in public relations*. Reprint, London: B.Y. Jove, 1990.

1.5 Historical books in online collections

If you are reading a scanned version of the printed book, complete with publication information and page numbers, reference in the same manner as the print book (see Section 1.1). Some early printed books do not have a publisher as they were privately printed. Record the information given in the book in your reference.

Citation order:

- Author/editor
- Year of publication (in round brackets)
- Title of publication (in italics)
- Place of publication and printing statement

Example

In-text citation

Adam's measured plans (Adam, 1764) …

Reference list

Adam, R. (1764) *Ruins of the palace of the Emperor Diocletian at Spalatro in Dalmatia*. London: Printed for the author.

1.6 Ancient texts

If citing an ancient text that existed before the invention of printing, reference it as a manuscript (see Section 25) or reference the published (and translated) edition you have read.

Citation order:

- Author
- Year of publication (in round brackets)
- Title of book (in italics)
- Translated by (if relevant)

- Edition (only include the edition number if it is not the first edition)
- Place of publication: publisher
- Series and volume number (where relevant)

Example

In-text citation

The classic tale by Homer (1991) …

Reference list

Homer (1991) *The Iliad*. Translated by R. Fagles. Introduction and notes by B. Knox. London: Penguin Books.

1.7 Translated books

Reference the translation you have read, not the original work.

Citation order:

- Author/editor
- Year of translated publication (in round brackets)
- Title of book (in italics)
- Translated by …
- Place of publication: reprint publisher

Example

In-text citation

Silone (1994) described peasant life in 1930s' Italy.

Reference list

Silone, I. (1994) *Fontamara*. Translated by G. David and E. Mosbacher. London: Redwords.

1.8 Books in languages other than English

If referencing a book in its original language, give the title exactly as shown in the book.

Citation order:
- Author/editor
- Year of publication (in round brackets)
- Title of book (in italics)
- Place of publication: publisher

Example

In-text citation

Her depiction of middle-class lifestyles (Beauvoir, 1966) …

Reference list

Beauvoir, S. de (1966) *Les Belles Images*. Paris: Gallimard.

1.9 Chapters/sections of edited books

Citation order:
- Author of the chapter/section (surname followed by initials)
- Year of publication (in round brackets)
- Title of chapter/section (in single quotation marks)
- 'in' plus author/editor of book
- Title of book (in italics)
- Place of publication: publisher
- Page reference

Example

In-text citation

The view proposed by Franklin (2012, p. 88) …

Reference list

Franklin, A.W. (2012) 'Management of the problem', in Smith, S.M. (ed.) *The maltreatment of children*. Lancaster: MTP, pp. 83–95.

1.10 Multi-volume works

1.10 a. Multi-volume works

Citation order:
- Author/editor
- Year of publication (in round brackets)
- Title of book (in italics)
- Volumes (in round brackets)
- Place of publication: publisher

Example

In-text citation

Butcher's (1961) guide …

Reference list

Butcher, R. (1961) *A new British flora* (2 vols). London: Leonard Hill.

When citing a *single volume of a multi-volume work,* add the title of the relevant volume to your **reference list**.

Example

In-text citation

Part 1 of Butcher's work (1961) …

Reference list

Butcher, R. (1961) *A new British flora. Part 1: lycopodiaceae to salicaceae*. London: Leonard Hill.

1.10 b. Chapters in multi-volume works

Citation order:

- Author of the chapter/section (surname followed by initials)
- Year of publication (in round brackets)
- Title of chapter/section (in single quotation marks)
- 'in' plus author/editor of book
- Title of book (in italics)
- Place of publication: publisher
- Page numbers of chapter/section

Example

In-text citation

In analysing ports (Jackson, 2000) …

Reference list

Jackson, G. (2000) 'Ports 1700–1840', in Clark, P. (ed.) *Cambridge urban history of Britain: Vol. 2 1540–1840*. Cambridge: Cambridge University Press, pp. 705–731.

1.10 c. Collected works

Citation order:

- Author/editor
- Year(s) of publication of collection (in round brackets)
- Title of book (in italics)
- Volumes (in round brackets)
- Place of publication: publisher

Example

In-text citation

His collected works (Jung, 1989–1995) provide …

Reference list

Jung, C.G. (1989–1995) *Gesammelte Werke* (24 vols). Olten: Walter Verlag.

1.11 Anthologies

Citation order:

- Editor/compiler of anthology (surname followed by initials)
- Year of publication (in round brackets)
- Title of book (in italics)
- Place of publication: publisher

Example

In-text citation

In his collection of humorous poems, West (1989) …

Reference list

West, C. (compiler and illustrator) (1989) *The beginner's book of bad behaviour*. London: Beaver Books.

For *a line of a poem/prayer within an anthology*, use the following citation order:

- Author of the poem/prayer (surname followed by initials)
- Year of publication (in round brackets)
- Title of poem/prayer (in single quotation marks)
- 'in' plus author/editor/compiler of book
- Title of book (in italics)
- Place of publication: publisher
- Page reference

Example

In-text citation

'The lion made a sudden stop
He let the dainty morsel drop' (Belloc, 1989, p. 89).

Reference list

Belloc, H. (1989) 'Jim', in West, C. (compiler and illustrator) *The beginner's book of bad behaviour*. London: Beaver Books, pp. 88–92.

1.12 Lines within plays

Citation order:

- Author (surname followed by initials)
- Year of publication (in round brackets)
- Title (in italics)
- Edition information
- Place of publication: publisher
- Act. Scene: line

Example

In-text citation

'I prithee do not mock me fellow student' (Shakespeare, 1980, 1.2: 177).

Reference list

Shakespeare, W. (1980) *Hamlet*. Edited by Spencer, T.J.B. London: Penguin. 1.2: 177.

NB If referencing a live performance, see Section 19.3.

1.13 Bibliographies

Although print **bibliographies** have been largely replaced by electronic sources for current information, they may provide commentary and highlight earlier writings.

Citation order:

- Author/editor
- Year of publication (in round brackets)
- Title (in italics)
- Edition (only include the edition number if it is not the first edition)
- Place of publication: publisher
- Series and volume number (where relevant)

Example

In-text citation

Ushpol (1958) noted the key research …

Reference list

Ushpol, R. (1958) *Select bibliography of South African autobiographies*. Cape Town: University of Cape Town, School of Librarianship.

1.14 Reference books

In many cases, reference material (for example dictionaries, encyclopedias, bibliographies) does not have an obvious author or editor, and is usually known and therefore cited by its title.

Citation order:

- As for Section 1.1 (Printed books)

Example: with author

In-text citation

Beal (2008, p. 171) identified …

Reference list

Beal, P. (2008) 'Folio', *A dictionary of English manuscript terminology: 1450 to 2000*. Oxford: Oxford University Press.

Example: with no author

In-text citation

The definition (*Collins beginner's German dictionary*, 2008, p. 21) …

Reference list

Collins beginner's German dictionary (2008) New York: Collins.

1.15 Online reference books

As with other print sources, a growing number of reference books are now available as ebooks. There are two examples given below. Example 1 is a printed book made available online. Reference this in the same manner as the printed version. Example 2 is a reference work that was published in print and online. The online version is being updated regularly; the print version will not be updated until a new edition is published. As with other examples where print and online versions exist, be careful to reference the version you have used, as example 2 shows how they can vary.

Citation order:

- As for Section 1.9 (Chapters/sections of edited books)

OR when online version differs from printed version by being updated regularly, replace publication details with:

- Available at: URL
- (Accessed: date)

See example 2 below.

Example 1: printed book made available online

In-text citation

The process of adaptation is difficult to detect (Rose, 2007, p. 19).

Reference list

Rose, M.R. (2007) 'Adaptation', in Levin, S.A. (ed.) *Encyclopedia of biodiversity*, pp. 17–23.

Example 2: printed reference work that is being updated online

In-text citation for print version

Rutherford's contribution (Badash, 2004) …

Reference list for print version

Badash, L. (2004) 'Rutherford, Ernest, Baron Rutherford of Nelson (1871–1937)', in *Oxford dictionary of national biography*. Oxford: Oxford University Press, pp. 381–389.

In-text citation for online version

Rutherford's contribution (Badash, 2008) …

Reference list for online version

which is being updated but print version is not

Badash, L. (2008) 'Rutherford, Ernest, Baron Rutherford of Nelson (1871–1937)', in *Oxford dictionary of national biography* (2004). Available at: http://www.oxforddnb.com/view/article/35891 (Accessed: 25 January 2013).

1.16 Sacred texts

1.16 a. The Bible

There is a well-established system for citing references from the Bible in your text. This uses the book name, chapter and verse (not page number, as this will vary between printings). It also avoids stating authors, as the actual authorship of some books is unclear.

NB The publisher and publication date are not required.

Citation order:

- Book of the Bible
- Chapter: verse
- Holy Bible (not in italics)
- Version of the Holy Bible

Example

In-text citation

The Beatitudes (Matthew 5: 3–12) …

Reference list

Matthew 5: 3–12, Holy Bible. New International Edition.

1.16 b. The Torah

Citation order:

- Torah (not in italics)
- Book
- Chapter: verse

Example

In-text citation

The reply (Shemot 3: 14) is the most profound …

Reference list

Torah. Shemot 3: 14.

1.16 c. The Qur'an

Citation order:

- Qur'an (not in italics)
- Surah (or chapter): verse
- Year of publication (in round brackets)
- Translated by …
- Place of publication: publisher

Example

In-text citation

'And ease for me my task' (Qur'an 20: 26).

Reference list

Qur'an 20: 26 (2010) Translated by Abdel Haleem, M.A.S. Oxford: Oxford University Press.

1.17 Atlases

NB See also Section 18.12 (Maps).

Citation order:

- As for Section 1.1 (Printed books)

Example

In-text citation

As illustrated in the text (*The Times comprehensive atlas of the world*, 2011, p. 201) …

Reference list

The Times comprehensive atlas of the world (2011) 13th edn. London: Times Books.

1.18   Pamphlets

Citation order:

- As for Section 1.1 (Printed books)

Example

In-text citation

Bradley's pamphlet (1994) gave instructions in the use of …

Reference list

Bradley, M. (1994) *CD-ROMs: how to set up your workstation*. London: ASLIB.

1.19   Exhibition catalogues

Citation order:

- Author of catalogue
- Year (in round brackets)
- Title of exhibition (in italics)
- Location and date(s) of exhibition
- [Exhibition catalogue]

Example

In-text citation

Urbach (2007, p. 8) noted the demands for reform …

Reference list

Urbach, P. (2007) *Reform! Reform! Reform!* Exhibition held at the Reform Club, London 2005–2006 and at Grey College, Durham University, March 2007 [Exhibition catalogue].

---

2.   Journal articles, print and electronic

Over recent years it has become clear that the referencing of journal articles, whether print or electronic, should be simplified. Given that the majority of journals are available online (via institutional databases, open access archives and *Google Scholar*), the inclusion of some reference elements listed in previous editions of *Cite them right* only serves to clutter the **reference**. Students and tutors can access academic journal articles through password-protected institutional databases, but other readers may not have access to these. Therefore, as long as the journal reference provides enough bibliographic information for the article to be located, other elements no longer need to be included, for example [Online], database title and **URL**. The reader would locate the article using the resources they can access and search.

If you are specifically referencing the *abstract* of a journal article, your **citation** would make this clear, for example: The abstract highlights … (Rodgers and Baker, 2013, p. 34). Note that the reference would follow the same format as for a journal article, as the page reference above would take the reader to the abstract.

NB If you wish to use a **Digital Object Identifier** (doi) (see Section D, pp. 16–17), follow the doi example given below.

2.1   Journal articles

Citation order:

- Author (surname followed by initials)
- Year of publication (in round brackets)
- Title of article (in single quotation marks)
- Title of journal (in italics – capitalise first letter of each word in title, except for linking words such as and, of, the, for)
- Issue information, that is, volume (unbracketed) and, where applicable, part number, month or season (all in round brackets)

- Title of journal (in italics – capitalise first letter of each word in title, except for linking words such as and, of, the, for)
- Issue information, that is, volume (unbracketed) and, where applicable, part number, month or season (all in round brackets)
- Page reference
- doi (if available)

Example: print or electronic journal article

In-text citation

In their review of the literature (Norrie *et al.*, 2012) …

Reference list

Norrie, C., Hammond, J., D'Avray, L., Collington, V. and Fook, J. (2012) 'Doing it differently? A review of literature on teaching reflective practice across health and social care professions', *Reflective Practice*, 13(4), pp. 565–578.

Example: electronic journal article with doi

In-text citation

Shirazi's review article (2010) …

Reference list

Shirazi, T. (2010) 'Successful teaching placements in secondary schools: achieving QTS practical handbooks', *European Journal of Teacher Education*, 33(3), pp. 323–326. doi: 10.1080/02619761003602246.

NB For prepublication articles, see Section 7.3.

2.2 Magazine articles

Citation order:
- As for journal articles in Section 2.1 above

Example

In-text citation

Bletcher discusses body image (2012, p. 9) …

Reference list

Bletcher, K. (2012) 'Matters of the heart', *Heart Matters* (August/September), pp. 9–11.

3. Newspaper articles, print and electronic

Just like journal articles, over recent years it has become clear that the referencing of newspaper articles, whether print or electronic, could be simplified. Students and tutors can access newspaper articles through password-protected institutional databases, but other readers may not have access to these. Therefore, as long as the newspaper reference provides enough bibliographic information for the article to be located, other elements no longer need to be included, for example [Online] and database title. The reader would locate the newspaper article using the format/resource they can access and search themselves.

Where the author (byline) of a newspaper article is identified, use the following citation order:
- Author/byline
- Year of publication (in round brackets)
- Title of article (in single quotation marks)

- Title of newspaper (in italics – capitalise first letter of each word in title, except for linking words such as and, of, the, for)
- Edition if required (in round brackets)
- Day and month
- Page reference

Example

In-text citation

Financial incentives were offered to graduates (Mansell and Bloom, 2012).

Reference list

Mansell, W. and Bloom, A. (2012) '£10,000 carrot to tempt physics experts', *The Guardian*, 20 June, p. 5.

When referencing a *regional newspaper*, include the edition to distinguish it from others with the same title.

Example

In-text citation

House prices fell by 2.1 per cent last month (Old, 2012).

Reference list

Old, D. (2012) 'House price gloom', *Evening Chronicle* (Newcastle edn), 26 June, p. 25.

Where no author (byline) is given, use the following citation order:
- Title of newspaper (in italics – capitalise first letter of each word in title, except for linking words such as and, of, the, for)
- Year of publication (in round brackets)
- Title of article (in single quotation marks)
- Day and month
- Page reference

Example

In-text citation

The article (*The Times*, 2012, p. 7) reported …

Reference list

The Times (2012) 'Bank accounts', 14 June, p. 7.

NB If you are specifically using the online version of a newspaper, often without pagination, then you would reference it as a *web page*, e.g. one with *individual authors*.

Example

In-text citation

US-led air strikes appeared to be imminent (Roberts and Ackerman, 2013).

Reference list

Roberts, D. and Ackerman, S. (2013) *US draft resolution allows Obama 90 days for military action against Syria*. Available at: http://www.theguardian.com/world/2013/sep/04/syria-strikes-draft-resolution-90-days (Accessed: 9 September 2013).

NB If you are citing several articles published in the same year, use a, b, c and so on after the year, for example *The Times* (2013a).

If you are referencing *letters* or *leading articles/editorials*, you would note this in your citations. When referencing a *section of a newspaper*, where page numbering may well be the same as in the main newspaper, give the section as a subtitle.

Example: letter

In-text citation

In their letter, Fells *et al.* (2011, p. 23) …

Reference list

Fells, I., Banks, T., Henry, E. and Lowther, G. (2011) 'Energise projects', *The Times*, 1 August, p. 23.

Example: leading article

In-text citation

In the leading article (*The Independent*, 2012, p. 28) …

Reference list

The Independent (2012) 'Grace in defeat', 27 January, p. 28.

Example: section

In-text citation

A recent article (*The Guardian*; *G2*, 2013, p. 14) …

Reference list

The Guardian: G2 (2013) 'Hope springs eternal', 24 July, p. 14.

4. Conferences

4.1 Full conference proceedings

Citation order:
- Author/editor
- Year of publication (in round brackets)
- Title of conference: subtitle (in italics)
- Location and date of conference
- Place of publication: publisher

Example

In-text citation

The conference (Institute for Small Business Affairs, 2000) …

Reference list

Institute for Small Business Affairs (2000) *Small firms: adding the spark: the 23rd ISBA national small firms policy and research conference*. Robert Gordon University, Aberdeen, 15–17 November. Leeds: Institute for Small Business Affairs.

4.2 Individual conference papers

Citation order:
- Author of paper
- Year of publication (in round brackets)
- Title of paper (in single quotation marks)
- Title of conference: subtitle (in italics)
- Location and date of conference
- Place of publication: publisher
- Page references for the paper

Example

In-text citation

Cook (2000) highlighted examples …

Reference list

Cook, D. (2000) 'Developing franchised business in Scotland', *Small firms: adding the spark: the 23rd ISBA national small firms policy and research conference*. Robert Gordon University, Aberdeen, 15–17 November. Leeds: Institute for Small Business Affairs, pp. 127–136.

4.3 Papers from conference proceedings published on the internet

Citation order:

- Author
- Year of publication (in round brackets)
- Title of paper (in single quotation marks)
- Title of conference: subtitle (in italics)
- Location and date of conference
- Publisher
- Available at: URL (or doi if available)
- (Accessed: date) (not required when doi used)

Example

In-text citation

A recent paper (Mendes and Romão, 2011) …

Reference list

Mendes, L. and Romão, T. (2011) 'Children as teachers', *Proceedings of the 8th international conference on advances in computer entertainment technology*, Lisbon, Portugal, 8–11 November. doi: 10.1145/2071423.2071438.

---

5. Unpublished and confidential information

Unpublished is generally understood as meaning 'not in the public domain'. This section includes a number of the most commonly used unpublished documents that students ask about. However, other material that could be deemed unpublished can be found under what are considered more relevant headings, for example Personal and virtual learning environments (Section 6), certain Visual sources (Section 18), Personal communications (Section 23) and Genealogical sources (Section 24).

5.1 Theses

Citation order:

- Author
- Year of submission (in round brackets)
- Title of thesis (in italics)
- Degree statement
- Degree-awarding body

OR if viewed online:

- Available at: URL
- (Accessed: date)

Examples

In-text citation

Research by Tregear (2001) and Parsons (2011) …

Reference list

Parsons, J.D. (2011) *Black holes with a twist.* PhD thesis. Durham University. Available at: http://etheses.dur.ac.uk/846 (Accessed: 14 August 2012).

Tregear, A.E.J. (2001) *Speciality regional foods in the UK: an investigation from the perspectives of marketing and social history.* Unpublished PhD thesis. Newcastle University.

5.2 Tutors' handouts

NB For tutors' lecture notes in virtual learning environments, see Section 6.1.

You should always check with your tutor whether or not you are allowed to refer to course materials and your own work. It is more academically correct to refer to published sources.

Citation order:

- Tutor
- Year of distribution (in round brackets)
- Title of handout (in single quotation marks)
- Module code: module title (in italics)
- Institution
- Unpublished

Example

In-text citation

The tutor's handout (Hadley, 2013) …

Reference list

Hadley, S. (2013) 'Biomechanics: introductory readings', *BM289: Sport biomechanics*. University of Cumbria. Unpublished.

5.3   Students' own work

Citation order:

- Student name
- Year of submission (in round brackets)
- Title of essay/assignment (in single quotation marks)
- Module code: module title (in italics)
- Institution
- Unpublished essay/assignment

Example

In-text citation

The topic of the essay (Sanders, 2012) …

Reference list

Sanders, M. (2012) 'An examination of the factors influencing air routes and the siting of international airports', *GEM5092: Geography and Environmental Management*. City University. Unpublished essay.

5.4   Internal reports

NB For published reports, see Section 11.

Citation order:

- Author or organisation
- Year produced (in round brackets)
- Title of report (in italics)
- Internal report (including name of institution)
- Unpublished

Example

In-text citation

Recommendations in the report (Harris, 2013) …

Reference list

Harris, G. (2013) *Focus group recommendations*. Internal LGU report. Unpublished.

5.5   Confidential information

In many cases you will need to anonymise the person or institution involved. In medical situations, for example, you may use terms such as 'Subject 1', 'Patient X' or 'Baby J' instead of real names; or 'Placement school', 'Placement hospital' or 'Placement agency' instead of actual institutions.

Citation order:

- Anonymised institution/agency (in square brackets)
- Year produced (in round brackets)
- Anonymised title (in italics) (use square brackets for the anonymised part)
- Location
- Anonymised producer (in square brackets)

If providing the town or city name is likely to identify a specific institution, you can simply insert the county, for example Lancashire: [Placement hospital].

Note that you may be asked by your tutor to supply them with the agency/employer name if there is any doubt about the authenticity of your reference.

NB See Section 18.5 d. for information relating to using and referencing medical images.

6. Personal and virtual learning environments, for example Blackboard, PebblePad, WebCT and Wimba

Personal learning environments/systems (such as PebblePad) are often known as 'eportfolios' or 'webfolios'. They generally include a collection of electronic information (coursework, images, multimedia, hyperlinks and other electronic files) demonstrating the student's learning record and evidence of achievements. In many cases, eportfolios are now retained within university **virtual learning environments** (VLEs; also known as online learning environments – OLEs), which means that they are not easily accessible to others outside the VLE. External hosts like PebblePad can offer solutions to this problem, although issues relating to confidential information may persist (see Section 5.5).

In eportfolios, a multitude of different types of information may be referenced. However, the reference will always relate to the web page of the user's/student's work. For more specific examples, see: http://www.pebblepad.co.uk/examples.asp.

VLEs and collaboration suites, for example Blackboard, WebCT and Wimba, are used in further and higher education as stores for course documents and teaching materials, and for discussion between tutors and students and between students. You will need to distinguish what you are citing, for example a tutor's notes, a journal article, text extracted from a book and digitised for use in VLEs, or an item from a discussion board. Note in the examples below that the URL is for the access point to the VLE, as a reader would need login details to locate the item being cited.

6.1 Tutors' lecture notes

NB For unpublished tutors' handouts, see Section 5.2; for lecture notes/presentations available on the **internet**, see Section 22.1.

Citation order:
- Author or tutor
- Year of publication (in round brackets)
- Title of item (in single quotation marks)
- Module code: module title (in italics)
- Available at: URL of VLE
- (Accessed: date)

Example

In-text citation

The need for preparation (Hollis, 2008) …

Reference list

Hollis, K. (2008) 'Week 7: dissertation preparation materials'. *HIST 4271:Research methods for MA History*. Available at: http://duo.dur.ac.uk (Accessed: 21 June 2012).

6.2   PowerPoint presentations

Citation order:
- Author or tutor
- Year of publication (in round brackets)
- Title of presentation (in single quotation marks)
- [PowerPoint presentation]
- Module code: module title (in italics)
- Available at: URL of VLE
- (Accessed: date)

Example

In-text citation

The excellent presentation (Booth, 2011) …

Reference list

Booth L. (2011) 'History of radiography' [PowerPoint presentation]. *MISR4004: Patient care skills: an introduction to human sciences*. Available at: https://mylearning.cumbria.ac.uk (Accessed: 7 August 2012).

6.3   Journal articles

Citation order:
- Author
- Year of publication (in round brackets)
- Title of article (in single quotation marks)
- Title of journal (in italics)
- Volume, issue, page numbers
- Module code: module title (in italics)
- Available at: URL of VLE
- (Accessed: date)

Example

In-text citation

Bright (2003, p. 262) believed …

Reference list

Bright, M. (2003) 'The advance of learning', *Journal of Ideas*, 46(2), pp. 259–277. *EDUC 1037: E-learning in the classroom*. Available at: http://duo.dur.ac.uk (Accessed: 23 July 2012).

6.4   Learning support materials

Sometimes you will access, and need to reference, material from modules not produced by tutors, for example skills modules produced by learning support teams.

Citation order:
- Author
- Year of publication (in round brackets)
- Title of item (in single quotation marks)
- Title of support/skills module (in italics): subtitle (if required) (in italics)
- Available at: URL of VLE
- (Accessed: date)

Example

In-text citation

… and this module allows you to test your own skills (University of Cumbria, Library and Student Services, 2012).

Reference list

University of Cumbria, Library and Student Services (2012) 'Skills evaluation tools', *Skills@cumbria: assess your skills.* Available at: https://mylearning.cumbria.ac.uk (Accessed: 18 July 2012).

6.5 Text extracts from books digitised for use in VLEs

Citation order:

- Author
- Year of publication of book (in round brackets)
- Extract title (in single quotation marks)
- 'in'
- Title of book (in italics)
- Place of publication: publisher (if available)
- Page numbers of extract
- Module code: module title (in italics)
- Available at: URL of VLE
- (Accessed: date)

Example

In-text citation

At least one author (Fenwick, 2007) …

Reference list

Fenwick, H. (2007) 'The Human Rights Act', in *Civil liberties and human rights*. London: Routledge Cavendish, pp. 157–298. *LAW 1032: Legal skills*. Available at: http://duo.dur.ac.uk (Accessed: 7 September 2012).

6.6 Messages from course discussion boards

Citation order:

- Author
- Year of publication (in round brackets)
- Title of message (in single quotation marks)
- Title of discussion board (in italics)
- 'in'
- Module code: module title (in italics)
- Available at: URL of VLE
- (Accessed: date)

Example

In-text citation

It is advisable to check which referencing style is required (Thomas, 2008).

Reference list

Thomas, D. (2008) 'Word count and referencing style', *Frequently Asked Questions discussion board*, in *PHYS 2011: Housing Studies*. Available at: http://duo.dur.ac.uk (Accessed: 14 October 2012).

7. Digital repositories

Many academic and learned institutions maintain digital repositories of the research undertaken by their members and make digital copies (eprints) of book chapters, journal articles and conference papers available via the internet. Digital repositories are useful sources of new research and are often heavily cited in scientific literature.

If the book or article has already been published, reference it as the publication. Repositories can also be used by authors to present their articles to readers before traditional publication processes, such as

peer-review, have been completed. Peer-review can take many months, by which time the value and opportunities raised by the new information may be lost. This form of rapid publication is common in the sciences, where early notice and discussion of new research is essential. If the articles are available before the item has been peer-reviewed, they are known as 'preprints'.

As with all internet-based sources, be clear what you are referencing. If it is a book, chapter or article that has already been published, reference it as you would the printed source, as in the book and conference paper examples below. If it is a prepublication article, conference, working paper or presentation that has not been peer-reviewed or formatted by publishers, or is a draft of a work that was published later, be clear that you are referencing the preprint, as this may be different from what is published later. Give the doi or URL and accessed date and use [preprint] to highlight to your reader that you have read the preprint not the final approved article.

7.1 Books in digital repositories

Reference books and journal articles in repositories as you would for print versions.

> **Example**
>
> **In-text citation**
> Previous PhD candidates provided useful advice (Cook and Crang, 1995).
>
> **Reference list**
> Cook, I. and Crang, M. (1995) *Doing ethnographies*. Norwich: Geobooks.

7.2 Conference papers in digital repositories

Citation order:
- Author
- Year of publication (in round brackets)
- Title of paper (in single quotation marks)
- Title of conference: subtitle (in italics)
- Organisation or company (if stated)
- Location and date of conference

> **Example**
>
> **In-text citation**
> Price (2001) disputed the theory …
>
> **Reference list**
> Price, P.B. (2001) 'Life in solid ice?' *Workshop on life in ancient ice*, Westin Salishan Lodge, Gleneden Beach, Oregon, 30 June to 2 July 2001.

7.3 Prepublication journal articles online or in digital repositories

Citation order:
- Author
- Year (in round brackets)
- Title of article (in single quotation marks)
- To be published in (if this is stated)
- Title of journal (in italics and capitalise first letter of each word in title, except for linking words such as and, of, the, for)
- Volume and issue numbers (if stated)
- [Preprint]
- Available at: URL
- (Accessed: date)

8.   The internet

When referencing information you have retrieved from the internet, *you must distinguish what you are referring to*. The internet is made up of journal articles, organisation internet sites, personal internet sites, government publications, images, company data, presentations – a vast range of material. Examples of how to reference individual sources, such as journal articles, ebooks and images, are given with the entries for those sources. You will find below examples of how to cite and reference internet sites or **web pages** produced by individuals and organisations.

The nature of what you are referring to will govern how you cite or reference it. You should aim to provide sufficient information for a reader to be able to locate your information source. As material on the internet can be removed or changed, you should also note the date when you accessed/viewed the information – it might not be there in a few months' time.

Remember to evaluate all internet information for accuracy, authority, currency, coverage and objectivity. The ability to publish information on the internet bears no relation to the author's academic abilities.

The defining element in referencing a web page is its Uniform Resource Locator, or URL. This should be included in your reference list, but *do not include the URL in your **in-text citation***, *unless this is the only piece of information you have*.

8.1   Web pages with individual authors

Citation order:

* Author
* Year that the site was published/last updated (in round brackets)
* Title of web page (in italics)
* Available at: URL
* (Accessed: date)

8.2 Web pages with organisations as authors

> **Example**
>
> **In-text citation**
>
> After identifying symptoms (National Health Service, 2012) …
>
> **Reference list**
>
> National Health Service (2012) *Check your symptoms.* Available at: http://www.nhsdirect.nhs.uk/checksymptoms (Accessed: 17 October 2012).

8.3 Web pages with no authors

Use the title of the web page.

> **Example**
>
> **In-text citation**
>
> Illustrations of the houses can be found online (*Palladio's Italian villas*, 2005).
>
> **Reference list**
>
> *Palladio's Italian villas* (2005) Available at: http://www.boglewood.com/palladio/ (Accessed: 23 August 2012).

8.4 Web pages with no authors or titles

If no author or title can be identified, you should use the web page's URL. It may be possible to shorten a very long URL, as long as the route remains clear, but it may be necessary to give the full URL even in your citation. If a web page has no author or title, you might question whether or not it is suitable for academic work.

> **Example**
>
> **In-text citation**
>
> Video files may need to be compressed (http://www.newmediarepublic.com/dvideo/compression.html, 2012).
>
> **Reference list**
>
> http://www.newmediarepublic.com/dvideo/compression.html (2012) (Accessed: 14 July 2012).

8.5 Web pages with no dates

If the web page has no obvious date of publication/revision, use the URL (no date) and the date you accessed the page. You might question how useful undated information is to your research as it may be out of date.

> **Example**
>
> **In-text citation**
>
> Compression may be required (http://www.newmediarepublic.com/dvideo/compression.html, no date).
>
> **Reference list**
>
> http://www.newmediarepublic.com/dvideo/compression.html (no date) (Accessed: 16 July 2012).

8.6 Blogs

Blogs (weblogs) are produced by individuals and organisations to provide updates on issues of interest or concern. Beware that, as blogs are someone's opinions, they may not provide objective, reasoned discussion of an issue. Use blogs in conjunction with reputable sources. Note that due to the informality of the internet, many authors give first names or aliases.

Use the name they have used in your reference.

Citation order:

- Author of message
- Year that the site was published/last updated (in round brackets)
- Title of message (in single quotation marks)
- Title of internet site (in italics)
- Day/month of posted message
- Available at: URL
- (Accessed: date)

> **Example**
>
> **In-text citation**
>
> Nick Robinson (2012) noted the 'Cameron Direct' phenomenon.
>
> **Reference list**
>
> Robinson, N. (2012) 'Cameron Direct', *Nick Robinson's newslog*, 4 June. Available at: http://www.bbc.co.uk/ blogs/nickrobinson/ (Accessed: 11 October 2012).

NB For the social networking/micro-blogging service *Twitter*, see Section 8.8.

8.7   Wikis

Wikis are collaborative websites in which several (usually unidentified) authors can add and edit the information presented. What you read today may have changed by tomorrow. There have also been instances of false information being presented, although wiki editors try to ensure that the information is authentic. If you are going to use information from a wiki, *make sure that it is thoroughly referenced*. As with other websites, if there are no authors or references given, the information is unlikely to be suitable for academic work. Evaluate wiki information against sources of proven academic quality such as books and journal articles.

Citation order:

- Title of article (in single quotation marks)
- Year that the site was published/last updated (in round brackets)
- Available at: URL
- (Accessed: date)

> **Example**
>
> **In-text citation**
>
> Telford introduced new techniques of bridge construction ('Thomas Telford', 2012).
>
> **Reference list**
>
> 'Thomas Telford' (2012) Available at: http://en.wikipedia.org/wiki/Thomas_ Telford (Accessed: 11 September 2012).

8.8   Social networking websites

Note that as these sites require registration and then acceptance by other members, it is suggested that the main web address be used. You may wish to include a copy of the member-to-member discussion you are referring to as an appendix to your work, so that readers without access to the original can read it.

8.8   a. *Facebook*

Citation order:

- Author
- Year that the page was published/last updated (in round brackets)
- Title of page (in italics)
- Day/month of posted message

- Available at: URL
- (Accessed: date)

> **Example**
>
> **In-text citation**
>
> The campaign had over 7,000 members in less than one week (*Tynemouth outdoor pool*, 2012).
>
> **Reference list**
>
> *Tynemouth outdoor pool* (2012) 29 August. Available at: https://www.facebook.com (Accessed: 31 August 2012).

NB For images seen through social media sites, see Section 18.6 c.

8.8   b. *Twitter*

Citation order:
- Author
- Year that the page was last updated (in round brackets)
- Day/month of posted message
- Available at: URL
- (Accessed: date)

> **Example**
>
> **In-text citation**
>
> One celebrity (Fry, 2012) tweeted messages of support.
>
> **Reference list**
>
> Fry, S. (2012) 13 January. Available at: https://twitter.com/stephenfry (Accessed: 18 December 2012).

9.   CD-ROMs or DVD-ROMs

Citation order:
- Title of publication (in italics)
- Year of publication (in round brackets)
- [CD-ROM] or [DVD-ROM]
- Producer (where identifiable)
- Available: publisher/distributor

> **Example**
>
> **In-text citation**
>
> The student made extensive use of an authoritative source (*World development indicators*, 2002) ...
>
> **Reference list**
>
> *World development indicators* (2002) [CD-ROM]. The World Bank Group. Available: SilverPlatter.

10.   Computer games and programs

10.1   Computer games

Citation order:
- Author (if given)
- Date (if given)
- Title of program (in italics and capitalise initial letters)
- [Computer game]
- Availability, that is, distributor, address, order number (if given)

OR if downloaded from the internet:
- URL
- (Downloaded: date)

10.2 Computer programs

Citation order:

- Author (if given)
- Date (if given)
- Title of program (in italics and capitalise initial letters)
- Version (in round brackets)
- [Computer program]
- Availability, that is, distributor, address, order number (if given)

OR if downloaded from the internet:

- URL
- (Downloaded: date)

11. Reports

NB For unpublished internal reports, see Section 5.4.

Citation order:

- Author or organisation
- Year of publication (in round brackets)
- Title of report (in italics)
- Place of publication: publisher

OR if accessed on the internet:

- Available at: URL
- (Accessed: date)

11.1 Research reports

11.2   Company annual reports

Example

In-text citation

The company's profits expanded (BSkyB Ltd, 2011) …

Reference list

BSkyB Ltd. (2011) *Annual report 2011*. Available at: http://annualreview2011. sky.com/_assets/downloads/PDF/SKY-AnnRep2011/Full_Annual_Report_2011. pdf (Accessed: 8 January 2013).

11.3   Market research reports from online databases

Example

In-text citation

Mintel Oxygen (2011) noted problems in the market …

Reference list

Mintel Oxygen (2011) 'Car insurance UK'. Available at: http://academic.mintel. com (Accessed: 5 January 2013).

NB The section of the report collection is given in single quotation marks.

11.4   Financial reports from online databases

Citation order:
- Publishing organisation
- Year of publication/last updated (in round brackets)
- Title of extract (in single quotation marks)
- Available at: URL
- (Accessed: date)

Example

In-text citation

BT's profit margin rose by over 2 per cent in the financial year 2010–2011 (Bureau van Dijk, 2012).

Reference list

Bureau van Dijk (2012) 'BT Group plc company report'. Available at: http:// fame.bvdep.com (Accessed: 5 January 2013).

12.   Legal material using the Harvard (author-date) style

In many instances there are established guidelines for referencing legal material, which are different to the procedures used in Harvard style. Some examples of how to cite and reference legal sources in Harvard style are given below.

12.1   Papers: House of Commons and House of Lords

Citation order:
- Parliament. House of …
- Year of publication (in round brackets)
- Title (in italics)
- Paper number (in round brackets). For House of Lords papers, the paper number is also in round brackets to distinguish it from identical House of Commons paper numbers (see example below)
- Place of publication: publisher

12.2   Hansard

Hansard is the official record of debates and speeches given in Parliament, as well as written answers to questions and written statements by ministers. A fully searchable version of Hansard from 1988 for the Commons and from 1995 for the Lords is available online at http://www.parliament.uk/business/publications/hansard/ (Accessed: 29 July 2012). For more information on the use of Hansard, see *Factsheet G17: The Official Report* (2010) produced by the House of Commons Information Office. Available at: http://www.parliament.uk/documents/upload/g17.pdf (Accessed: 29 July 2012). We suggest adding the URL for the debate you are citing so that your reader can locate the precise section.

Citation order:

- Abbreviation of House and Deb (for Debates)
- Date of debate
- Volume number
- Column number
- Available at: URL
- (Accessed: date)

- If quoting very old Hansards, it is usual, although optional, to include the series number:

HC Deb (5th series) 13 January 1907, vol 878, cols 69–70

- In 2007, the earlier system of Standing Committees was replaced by Public Bill Committees. Standing Committee Hansard should be cited as follows:

SC Deb (A) 13 May 1998, col 345

The new Public Bill Committees would be cited thus:

Health Bill Deb 30 January 2007, cols 12–15

unless the Bill title is so long that this becomes ridiculous. In this case use:

PBC Deb (Bill 99) 30 January 2007, cols 12–15

or, where the context makes the Bill obvious:

PBC Deb 30 January 2007, cols 12–15.

12.3 Bills: House of Commons and House of Lords

Citation order:
- Parliament. House of …
- Year of publication (in round brackets)
- Title (in italics)
- Bill number (in brackets)
- Place of publication: publisher

Example

In-text citation

Haulage companies expressed concern about the provisions of the *Transport Bill* (Parliament. House of Commons, 1999).

Reference list

Parliament. House of Commons (1999) *Transport Bill* (Bills 1999–2000 8). London: The Stationery Office.

12.4 UK statutes (Acts of Parliament)

A major change in the citation of UK legal sources took place in 1963. Before this, an Act was cited according to the regnal year (that is, the number of years since the monarch's accession).

For *pre-1963 statutes*, use

Citation order:
- Short title of Act and year (in italics)
- Regnal year, name of sovereign and chapter number (in round brackets)
- Title of collection (in italics)
- Year of publication (in round brackets)
- Edition (only include edition number if it is not the first edition)
- Place of publication: publisher

Example: pre-1963 Act

In-text citation

With the *Act of Supremacy 1534* (26 Hen. 8, c. 1) …

Reference list

Act of Supremacy 1534 (26 Hen. 8, c. 1). *The Statutes* (1950) 3rd edn. London: HMSO.

For *post-1963 statutes*, use the short title of an Act, with the year in which it was enacted. Most Acts and parts of Acts are now available and viewed online, so reference the website where you located the Act.

NB As the date appears in the title of the Acts, there is no need to repeat the date in round brackets after the title.

If you are referencing legislation from more than one country (jurisdiction), include the country (jurisdiction) in round brackets after the title of the legislation (see examples in Section 12.6).

Citation order:
- Title of Act including year and chapter number (in italics)
- Country/jurisdiction (only if referencing more than one country's legislation)
- Available at: URL
- (Accessed: date)

Examples: post-1963 Act

In-text citation

In chapter 7 of recent social care legislation (*Health and Social Care Act 2012*) ...

Reference list

Health and Social Care Act 2012, c. 7. Available at: http://www.legislation.gov. uk/ukpga/2012/7/contents/enacted (Accessed: 23 August 2012).

OR if you use the pdf version:

Available at: http://www.legislation.gov. uk/ukpga/2012/7/pdfs/ ukpga_20120007_en.pdf (Accessed: 23 August 2012).

Example: section of an Act

In-text citation

Authority, as defined in section 10(4)(6) of the Act (*Children Act 2004*) ...

Reference list

Children Act 2004, c. 31. Available at: http://www.legislation.gov.uk/ukpga/ 2004/31/contents (Accessed: 29 August 2012).

12.5 Statutory Instruments (SIs)

Citation order:
- Name/title including year (in italics)
- SI year and number (in round brackets)
- Available at: URL
- (Accessed date)

Example

In-text citation

The *Terrorism (United Nations Measures) Order 2001* ...

Reference list

Terrorism (United Nations Measures) Order 2001 (SI 2001/3365). Available at: http://www.legislation.gov.uk/uksi/2001/ 3365/contents/made (Accessed: 23 December 2012).

12.6 Legislation from UK devolved Assemblies

12.6 a. Acts of the Scottish Parliament

For Acts of the post-devolution Scottish Parliament, replace the chapter number with 'asp' (meaning Act of the Scottish Parliament).

NB Legislation from UK devolved Assemblies is available online.

Citation order:

- Title of Act including year (in italics)
- asp number (in round brackets)
- Available at: URL
- (Accessed: date)

Example

In-text citation

In the legislation (*Budget (Scotland) Act 2004*) …

Reference list

Budget (Scotland) Act 2004 (asp 2). Available at: http://www.legislation.gov.uk/asp/2004/2/contents (Accessed: 29 August 2012).

12.6   b. Scottish Statutory Instruments (SSIs)

Citation order:

- Title of SSI including year (in italics)
- SSI number
- Available at: URL
- (Accessed: date)

Example

In-text citation

In the SSI of 2005 (*Tuberculosis (Scotland) Order 2005*) …

Reference list

Tuberculosis (Scotland) Order 2005, SSI 2005/434. Available at: http://www.legislation.gov.uk/ssi/2005/434/contents/made (Accessed: 29 August 2012).

12.6   c. Acts of the Northern Ireland Assembly

Citation order:

- Title of Act (Northern Ireland) including year (in italics)
- Available at: URL
- (Accessed: date)

Example

In-text citation

… which was discussed in the legislation (*Ground Rents Act (Northern Ireland) 2001*).

Reference list

Ground Rents Act (Northern Ireland) 2001. Available at: http://www.legislation.gov.uk/nia/2001/5/contents (Accessed: 29 August 2012).

12.6   d. Statutory Rules of Northern Ireland

The Northern Ireland Assembly may pass Statutory Instruments. These are called Statutory Rules of Northern Ireland.

Citation order:

- Title of Rule (Northern Ireland) including year (in italics)
- SR year/number
- Available at: URL
- (Accessed: date)

Example

In-text citation

The rules relating to flavourings (*Smoke Flavourings Regulations (Northern Ireland) 2005*) ...

Reference list

Smoke Flavourings Regulations (Northern Ireland) 2005, SR 2005/76. Available at: http://www.legislation.gov.uk/nisr/2005/76/contents/made (Accessed: 29 August 2012).

12.6   e. National Assembly for Wales legislation

The National Assembly for Wales may pass Assembly Measures (nawm), which are primary legislation but are subordinate to UK statutes.

Citation order:
- Title of Assembly Measure including year (in italics)
- (nawm number)
- Available at: URL
- (Accessed: date)

Example

In-text citation

The 2008 Measure (*NHS Redress (Wales) Measure 2008*) ...

Reference list

NHS Redress (Wales) Measure 2008 (nawm 1). Available at: http://www.legislation.gov.uk/mwa/2008/1/2008-07-09 (Accessed: 29 August 2012).

The National Assembly for Wales may also pass Statutory Instruments. As well as the SI number and year, Welsh Statutory Instruments have a W. number.

Citation order:
- Title of Order (Wales) including year (in italics)
- Welsh Statutory Instrument year/SI number (W. number)
- Available at: URL
- (Accessed: date)

Example

In-text citation

The Welsh Statutory Instrument (*The Bluetongue (Wales) Order 2003*) ...

Reference list

The Bluetongue (Wales) Order 2003 Welsh Statutory Instrument 2003/326 (W. 47). Available at: http://www.legislation.gov.uk/wsi/2003/326/contents/made (Accessed: 29 August 2012).

12.7   Law Commission reports and consultation papers

Citation order:
- Law Commission
- Year of publication (in round brackets)
- Title of report or consultation paper (in italics)
- Number of report or consultation paper, Command Paper number (if given) (in round brackets)
- Place of publication: publisher

OR if viewed online:
- Available at: URL
- (Accessed: date)

In-text citation

The report (Law Commission, 2001) recommended that retrial after acquittal should be permitted in cases of murder, if new evidence became available.

Reference list

Law Commission (2001) *Double Jeopardy and Prosecution Appeals.* (Law Com No 267, Cm 5048). London: The Stationery Office.

Law Commission (2001) *Double Jeopardy and Prosecution Appeals.* (Law Com No 267, Cm 5048). Available at: http://lawcommission.justice.gov.uk/areas/doublejeopardy.htm (Accessed: 29 August 2012).

12.8   Legal cases

In the United Kingdom there are distinct guidelines for the citing of legal sources such as court cases. These are set out in a citation system called OSCOLA (Oxford University Standard for Citation of Legal Authorities). See Section I for more information. These guidelines do not conform to the usual author-date format and in many instances use square brackets around the date. However, some law reports have several volumes for each year, in which case the date is enclosed in round brackets. Also, the case name is italicised but the publication name is not. For details of the accepted abbreviations for legal publications, see the Cardiff University *Cardiff index to legal abbreviations* at http://www.legalabbrevs.cardiff.ac.uk/.

Citation order:
* Name of parties involved in the case (in italics)
* Date
* Volume number (if used), abbreviation for name of report and first page of report

Examples

In-text citation

The cases of *R v. Dunlop* [2006] and *R v. Edwards (John)* (1991) upheld …

Reference list

R v. Dunlop [2006] EWCA Crim 1354

NB Date in square brackets in accordance with the convention used for legal material.

R v. Edwards (John) (1991) 93 Cr App R 48

NB Date in round brackets because there is also a volume number.

Citing names of judges

If you wish to quote something said by a judge, include their name in the in-text citation. If the judge is a peer, you would write, for example, 'Lord Blackstone'. If the judge is a Mr, Mrs or Ms, you would write 'Blackstone J' (J for judge); if a Lord Justice or Lady Justice, you would write 'Blackstone LJ'.

Example

In-text citation

In *R v. Jones* [2009] Williams LJ noted …

Reference list

R v. Jones [2009] EWCA Crim 120

13. Government publications

Government publications include Green and White Papers (published as Command Papers), which propose policies, and publications by individual departments giving advice or information.

13.1 Command Papers including Green and White Papers

Citation order:

- Name of committee or Royal Commission
- Year of publication (in round brackets)
- Title (in italics)
- Place of publication: publisher
- Paper number (in brackets)

OR if viewed online:

- Paper number (in round brackets after title)
- Available at: URL
- (Accessed: date)

Example

In-text citation

Useful advice (Lord Chancellor's Department, 1999; Ministry of Justice, 2013) …

Reference list

Lord Chancellor's Department (1999) *Government policy on archives*. London: The Stationery Office (Cm 4516).

Ministry of Justice (2013) *Transforming rehabilitation: a strategy for reform* (Cm 8619). Available at: http://www. official-documents.gov.uk/document/ cm86/8619/8619.pdf (Accessed: 16 May 2013).

13.2 Departmental publications

Citation order:

- Name of government department
- Year of publication (in round brackets)
- Title (in italics)
- Place of publication: publisher
- Series (in brackets) – if applicable

OR if viewed online:

- Available at: URL
- (Accessed: date)

Examples

In-text citations

Prison numbers increased last year (Ministry of Justice, 2007) as did the disparity in medical care (Department of Health, 2004; 2008).

Reference list

Department of Health (2004) *Primary medical services allocations 2004/05*. Health Service Circular HSC 2004/003. Available at: http://www.dh.gov.uk/en/ Publicationsandstatistics/ Lettersandcirculars/ Healthservicecirculars/DH_4071269 (Accessed: 21 June 2013).

Department of Health (2008) *Health inequalities: progress and next steps*. Available at: http://www.dh.gov.uk/en/ Publicationsandstatistics/Publications/ PublicationsPolicyAndGuidance/ DH_085307 (Accessed: 18 June 2013).

Ministry of Justice (2007) *Sentencing statistics* (*annual*). Available at: http:// www.justice.gov.uk/publications/ sentencingannual.htm (Accessed: 3 June 2013).

NB If you are referencing government publications from more than one country, include the country of origin (in round brackets) after the department name.

> **Example**
>
> **In-text citation**
>
> Canada has taken a tough stance on landmines (Department of Foreign Affairs and International Trade (Canada), 2012).
>
> **Reference list**
>
> Department of Foreign Affairs and International Trade (Canada) (2012) *Re-affirming the commitment*. Available at: http://www.international.gc.ca/mines/documents/cnd-fund-fond-can/00-01-introduction.aspx?lang=eng&view=d (Accessed: 5 January 2013).

> **Examples**
>
> **In-text citation**
>
> Reports by the United Nations (2011) and International Chamber of Commerce, Commission for Air Transport (2010) …
>
> **Reference list**
>
> International Chamber of Commerce, Commission for Air Transport (2010) *The need for greater liberalization in international air transport*. Available at: http://www.iccwbo.org/Advocacy-Codes-and-Rules/Document-centre/2009/The-need-for-greater-liberalization-of-international-air-transport/ (Accessed: 9 February 2013).
>
> United Nations (2011) *Yearbook of the United Nations, 2007 vol. 61*. New York: United Nations Department of Public Information.

14. Publications of international organisations

Citation order:
- Name of organisation or institution
- Year of publication (in round brackets)
- Title (in italics)
- Place of publication: publisher

OR if viewed online:
- Available at: URL
- (Accessed: date)

15. European Union (EU) publications

Citation order:
- Name of EU institution (for example, Council of the European Union, European Commission)
- Year of publication (in round brackets)
- Title (in italics)
- Place of publication: publisher

> **Example**
>
> **In-text citation**
>
> The predicted migration of labour (European Commission, 2003) …
>
> **Reference list**
>
> European Commission (2003) *Making globalisation work for everyone*. Luxembourg: Office for Official Publications of the European Communities.

16. Scientific and technical information

16.1 British Standards

Citation order:
- Name of authorising organisation
- Year of publication (in round brackets)
- Number and title of standard (in italics)
- Place of publication: publisher

OR if viewed online:
- Available at: URL
- (Accessed: date)

Examples

In-text citation

Loft conversions are subject to strict controls (British Standards Institution, 1989).

Reference list

British Standards Institution (1989) *BS5268-7.4: Structural use of timber: ceiling binders*. London: British Standards Institution.

British Standards Institution (1989) *BS5268-7.4: Structural use of timber: ceiling binders*. Available at: http://www.standardsuk.com/ (Accessed: 30 June 2012).

16.2 Patents

Citation order:
- Inventor(s)
- Year of publication (in round brackets)
- Title (in italics)
- Authorising organisation
- Patent number
- Available at: URL
- (Accessed: date)

Example

In-text citation

Padley (2012) proposed a solution.

Reference list

Padley, S. (2012) *Radiator isolating valve*. UK Intellectual Property Office Patent no. GB2463069. Available at: http://www.ipo.gov.uk/p-find-publication (Accessed: 24 August 2012).

16.3 Scientific datasets

Reference where you located the data, for example journal article/book/online.

Citation order:
- Author
- Date (in round brackets)
- Title of data (in single quotation marks)
- Available at: URL
- (Accessed: date)

Example

In-text citation

The data (Ralchenko *et al.*, 2009) proved …

Reference list

Ralchenko, Y., Kramida, A.E., Reader, J., and NIST ASD Team (2009) 'Na levels holdings'. Available at: http://physics.nist.gov/asd3 (Accessed: 2 August 2012).

16.4 Requests For Comments (RFCs)

Citation order:
- Author/editor
- Year (in round brackets)
- Title (in italics)

- Document number
- Available at: URL
- (Accessed: date)

Example

In-text citation

A number of comments were made relating to the document (Hoffman and Harris, 2006).

Reference list

Hoffman, P. and Harris, S. (2006) *The Tao of IETF: a novice's guide to the Internet Engineering Task Force.* Nos: FYI 17 and RFC 4677. Available at: http://tools.ietf.org/html/rfc4677 (Accessed: 20 October 2012).

16.5 Mathematical equations

Reference where you located the equation, for example online journal article.

Citation order:
- Author
- Year of publication (in round brackets)
- Title of article (in single quotation marks)
- Title of journal (in italics – capitalise first letter of each word in title, except for linking words such as and, of, the, for)
- Volume, issue, page numbers
- Available at: URL (or doi if available)
- (Accessed: date) (not required when doi used)

Example

In-text citation

Fradelizi and Meyer (2008, p. 1449) noted that for z>0

$$P(K) \geq \frac{e^{n+1-z}z^{n+1}}{(n!)^2}$$

Reference list

Fradelizi, M. and Meyer, M. (2008) 'Some functional inverse Santaló inequalities', *Advances in Mathematics*, 218(5), pp. 1430–1452. doi: 10.1016/j.aim.2008.03.013.

16.6 Graphs

Reference where you located the graph, for example graph in a book (give book details).

Citation order:
- Author
- Year of publication (in round brackets)
- Title of book (in italics)
- Place of publication: publisher
- Page number or figure number for graph
- Graph

Example

In-text citation

The effects of the compounds (Day and Gastel, 2006, p. 95) …

Reference list

Day, R. and Gastel, B. (2006) *How to write and publish a scientific paper.* Cambridge: Cambridge University Press, p. 95, graph.

---

17. Reviews

Citation order:

- Name of the reviewer (if indicated)
- Year of publication of the review (in round brackets)
- Title of the review (in single quotation marks)
- Review of … (title of work reviewed – in italics)
- Author/director of work being reviewed
- Publication details (title in italics)

17.1 Book reviews

Example

In-text citation

Darden (2007) considered the book …

Reference list

Darden, L. (2007) 'New cell research'. Review of *Discovering cell mechanisms: the creation of modern cell biology*, by William Bechtel. *Journal of the History of Biology*, 40(1), pp. 185–187.

17.2 Drama reviews

Example

In-text citation

One reviewer (Billington, 2008, p. 19) wrote …

Reference list

Billington, M. (2008) 'The main event'. Review of *On the rocks*, by D.H. Lawrence. Hampstead Theatre, London. *The Guardian* (Review section), 5 July, p. 19.

17.3 Film reviews

Examples

In-text citation

Barnes (1989) and Parsons (2010) thought it a classic film.

Reference list

Example: magazine review

Barnes, L. (1989) 'Citizen Kane'. Review of *Citizen Kane*, directed by Orson Welles (RKO). *New Vision*, 9 October, pp. 24–25.

Example: internet review

Parsons, T. (2010) 'A rosebud by any other name'. Review of *Citizen Kane*, directed by Orson Welles. Available at: http://www.imdb.com/title/tt0033467/reviews?start=210 (Accessed: 5 July 2012).

17.4 Reviews of musical performances

Example

In-text citation

Hickling (2008) thought it 'a little touch of magic'.

Reference list

Hickling, A. (2008) 'The opera'. Review of *Don Giovanni*, by Mozart, New Vic, Newcastle-under-Lyme. *The Guardian* (Review section), 5 July, p. 19.

18. Visual sources

The internet has revolutionised the availability of visual sources such as images, maps and artistic works. Some examples below will show how to cite and reference the original works and online versions.

18.1 Exhibitions

Citation order:

- Title of exhibition (in italics)
- Year (in round brackets)
- [Exhibition]
- Location. Date(s) of exhibition

> **Example**
>
> **In-text citation**
> The acclaimed exhibition in London is one of the finest (*Pre-Raphaelites: Victorian Avant-Garde*, 2012).
>
> **Reference list**
> *Pre-Raphaelites: Victorian Avant-Garde* (2012) [Exhibition]. Tate Britain, London. 12 September 2012–13 January 2013.

18.2 Paintings/drawings

Citation order:

- Artist
- Year (if available)
- Title of the work (in italics)
- Medium (in square brackets)
- Institution or collection that houses the work, followed by the city

OR if seen online:

- Available at:
- (Accessed: date)

> **Examples**
>
> **In-text citation**
> Works by Coello (1664) and Dalí (1958) …
>
> **Reference list**
> Coello, C. (1664) *The triumph of St Augustine* [Oil on canvas]. Museo del Prado, Madrid.
>
> Dalí, S. (1958) *Madonna* [Oil on canvas]. Available at: http://www.oxfordartonline.com (Accessed: 9 July 2012).

18.3 Sculpture, statues and memorials

18.3 a. Sculpture

Citation order:

- Sculptor
- Year (in round brackets)
- Title (in italics)
- [Sculpture]
- Gallery or name of collection

OR if viewed online, add:
- Available at: URL
- (Accessed: date)

> **Example**
>
> **In-text citation**
>
> His talents were proven with *The lovers* (Rodin, 1886).
>
> **Reference list**
>
> Rodin, A. (1886) *The lovers* [Sculpture]. Private collection.

18.3 b. Statues

Citation order:
- Sculptor
- Year (in round brackets)
- Title (in italics)
- [Statue]
- Location (and/or GPS coordinates, if available)
- Date viewed (in round brackets)

> **Example**
>
> **In-text citation**
>
> The admiral's statue (Melton 2000) looks across the Channel to France.
>
> **Reference list**
>
> Melton, S. (2000) *Admiral Sir Bertram Home Ramsey* [Statue]. Dover Castle, Kent, England, GPS coordinates: 51° 7' 36.29" N, 1° 19' 26.22" E. (Viewed: 8 August 2012).

18.3 c. War memorials

Citation order:
- Name of architect (if known); if not, use name of memorial
- Date of construction (in round brackets)

- Name of memorial (in italics)
- Location (and/or GPS coordinates, if available)
- Date viewed (in round brackets)

> **Example**
>
> **In-text citation**
>
> The memorial (Leong Swee Lim, 1967) …
>
> **Reference list**
>
> Leong Swee Lim (1967) *Civilian War Memorial*, War Memorial Park, Beach Road, Singapore, GPS coordinates: 1° 17' 32.91" N, 103° 51' 11.11" E. (Viewed: 4 February 2012).

18.4 Inscriptions

18.4 a. Inscriptions on monuments

Inscriptions on gravestones and memorials are, in many instances, the only detailed record of a person's existence, circumstances and relationships, apart from basic information given in birth, marriage and death certificates and the census. Referencing this information can be difficult, but (as with printed information) you should aim to provide as much information as possible for another person to locate the gravestone or memorial. In some instances, the plot number of a grave will be obtainable and can be referenced; if not, try to give an indication of the location from a landmark.

Citation order:
- Name of deceased (in single quotation marks)
- Year of death/event (in round brackets)
- [Monument inscription]
- Location
- Date viewed (in round brackets)

Examples

In-text citation

The gravestone of the railway engineman ('Oswald Gardiner', 1840) compares him to one of the locomotives he drove: 'My engine now is cold and still. No water does my boiler fill.'

Reference list

'Oswald Gardiner' (1840) [Monument inscription] St Mary the Virgin Churchyard (5m northwest of church), Whickham, Tyne and Wear (Viewed: 12 August 2012).

Reference list

where plot number available

'Wilfred Pears' (1940) [Monument inscription] Plot 13, row E, grave 13, London Cemetery and Extension, Longueval, France. (Viewed: 25 August 2011).

18.4   b. Inscriptions on statues

Referencing inscriptions on statues can also be difficult, as the author may not be identified and the wording may be a quotation from an earlier source. Give as much information as you are able to.

Citation order:

- Author (if known); if not, use title of statue (in italics)
- Year of inscription (in round brackets)
- Inscription on statue to/of … (in italics)
- Location
- Date viewed (in round brackets)

Example

In-text citation

The inscription by Herbert (2000) …

Reference list

Herbert, A.P. (2000) *Inscription on statue to Admiral Bertram Home Ramsey*, Dover Castle, Kent, England. (Viewed: 8 August 2012).

18.4   c. Inscriptions on buildings

Citation order:

- Author (if known); if not, use first three words of inscription
- Year of inscription (in round brackets)
- Inscription on … (in italics)
- Location
- Date viewed (in round brackets)

Example

In-text citation

The exterior inscription by Lewis (2004) …

Reference list

Lewis, G. (2004) *Inscription on Wales Millennium Centre*, Cardiff Bay, Cardiff, Wales. (Viewed: 8 August 2012).

18.5   Displays

18.5   a. Installations/exhibits

Citation order:

- Artist
- Year (in round brackets)
- Title of installation or exhibit (in italics)
- [Installation] or [Exhibit]
- Gallery or location
- Date viewed

18.5   b. Graffiti

By its nature, graffiti is anonymous (even when the graffitist includes their signature tag). It is usually short-lived artistic expression (or vandalism, depending on one's perspective). As it may be removed at any time, it is essential to include as much information as possible to describe the content, location and date viewed. Be careful if citing offensive language or imagery in graffiti.

Citation order:

- Title or description (with graffitist's tag, if present) (in italics)
- Year (in round brackets)
- [Graffiti]
- Location
- Date viewed

18.6   Photographs/images

Students often become confused when referencing works of art they have photographed. They are often unsure whether to reference themselves as the image maker or to reference the work itself. The answer is clear: you reference what it is you are referring to (ie your photograph or the work of art). Thus, if you wish to discuss the way you photographed a sculpture by Rodin, you would reference yourself, following the examples below (omitting, if necessary, place of publication and publisher). If, however, you photographed Rodin's sculpture in a gallery and you are discussing the sculpture itself, you would follow the guidelines in Sections 18.2 or 18.4.

NB For images that you download onto edevices, and to which you still have access, you should replace accessed date with downloaded date.

18.6   a. Prints or slides

Citation order:

- Photographer
- Year (in round brackets)
- Title of photograph (in italics)
- [Photograph]
- Place of publication: publisher (if available)

> ### Example
>
> **In-text citation**
>
> The seasonal and architectural changes were captured on film (Thomas, 2003).
>
> **Reference list**
>
> Thomas, T. (2003) *Redevelopment in Newcastle* [Photograph]. Newcastle upon Tyne: Then & Now Publishing.

18.6   b. Photographs from the internet

Citation order:

- Photographer
- Year of publication (in round brackets)
- Title of photograph (in italics)
- Available at: URL
- (Accessed/downloaded: date)

> ### Example
>
> **In-text citation**
>
> His beautiful photograph (Kitto, 2008) …
>
> **Reference list**
>
> Kitto, J. (2008) *Golden sunset*. Available at: http://www.jameskitto.co.uk/photo_1827786.html (Accessed: 14 June 2012).

18.6   c. Photographs in online collections

On occasions, you may need to reference images that you have found through social media sites like *Pinterest* or *Tumblr*, or that you have viewed directly on *Flickr*. Do not be confused: you simply take the reader to where you viewed the image.

Citation order:

- Photographer
- Year of publication (in round brackets)
- Title of photograph (in italics)
- Available at: URL
- (Accessed/Downloaded: date)

> ### Example: *Tumblr*
>
> **In-text citation**
>
> Solar ikon's recent work (2012) …
>
> **Reference list**
>
> Solar ikon (2012) *Green onion*. Available at: http://www.tumblr.com/tagged/food (Accessed: 13 June 2012).

> ### Example: *Flickr*
>
> **In-text citation**
>
> Chunyang Lin's (Solar ikon) recent work (2012) …
>
> **Reference list**
>
> Lin, C. (2012) *Green onion*. Available at: http://www.flickr.com/photos/chunyang/4004866489/ (Downloaded: 13 June 2012).

18.6 d. Medical images

Many kinds of medical/anatomical images can be viewed and downloaded from the internet (for example, MRI, PET, CT and ultrasound scans and X-rays) for use in supporting your arguments or demonstrating particular aspects of anatomical or medical information. These would simply be referenced as photographs/images from the internet (see Section 18.5 b. above).

Other images may be found in online databases such as *Anatomy TV*. For these, use the following format.

Citation order:
- Image title (in italics)
- Year (in round brackets)
- Medium (in square brackets)
- Available at: URL
- (Accessed/Downloaded: date)

Example

In-text citation

The X-ray and scan (2013) clearly showed …

Reference list

The spine (2013) [X-ray and MRI scan]. Available at: http://www.anatomy.tv/new_home.aspx (Accessed: 28 July 2013).

However, if you are working on placement in a hospital, there will be occasions when you may want to reference an individual patient's scan, for example. These are confidential sources of information, and as such these images would need to be anonymised (as shown in Section 5.5), and the patient's and hospital's permission given if you wanted to use the image in your text/appendices. In these circumstances, use the following format.

Citation order:
- Anonymised patient's name (in square brackets)
- Year image produced (in round brackets)
- Image title (in italics)
- Medium (in square brackets)
- Location
- Institution

Example

In-text citation

The patient's X-ray (2012) …

Reference list

[Patient Y] (2012) *Left knee joint* [X-ray]. Bradford: Bradford Royal Infirmary.

18.7   Packaging

Citation order:
- Manufacturer
- Year seen
- Product name (in italics)
- Medium (in square brackets)

OR if seen online, add:
- Available at: URL
- (Accessed: date)

In-text citation

The different forms of packaging (The Premier Foods Group, 2012; Mars Incorporated, 2013) …

Reference list

Mars Incorporated (2013) *Mars Bar* [Wrapper].

The Premier Foods Group (2012) *Loyd Grossman tomato and mushroom sauce* [Jar label]. Available at: www.loydgrossmansauces.co.uk (Accessed: 23 May 2012).

18.8   Book illustrations, figures, diagrams, logos and tables

Citation order:

- Author of book
- Year of publication (in round brackets)
- Title of book (in italics)
- Place of publication: publisher
- Page reference of illustration and so on
- illus./fig./diagram/logo/table

Example

In-text citation

Holbein's painting illustrated the prelate's ornate mitre (Strong, 1990, pp. 62–63).

Reference list

Strong, R. (1990) *Lost treasures of Britain*. London: Viking, pp. 62–63, illus.

OR if seen online, reference as shown in Sections 8.1/8.2 and add Medium (in square brackets).

Example

In-text citation

Controversy has surrounded the Olympic logo (London2012, 2010) …

Reference list

London2012 (2010) *London2012* [Logo]. Available at: http://www.london2012.com (Accessed: 23 May 2012).

18.9   Cartoons

Citation order:

- Artist
- Date (if available)
- Title of cartoon (in single quotation marks)
- [Cartoon]
- Title of publication (in italics)
- Day and month

OR if seen online add:

- Available at: URL
- (Accessed: date)

Example

In-text citation

Steve Bell (2008) warned of the danger …

Reference list

Bell, S. (2008) 'Don't let this happen' [Cartoon]. *The Guardian*, 19 June. Available at: http://www.guardian.co.uk/world/cartoon/2008/jun/19/steve.bell.afghanistan.troops (Accessed: 2 July 2012).

18.10 Comic strips

Citation order:

- Author (where available)
- Title of comic strip (in single quotation marks)
- Year of publication (in round brackets)
- Title of comic (in italics)
- Day, month, page

Example

In-text citation

Jessica Ennis starred as Ennis the Menace in the hilarious comic strip ('The menace heptathlon', 2012).

Reference list

'The menace heptathlon' (2012) *The Beano*, 25 August, pp. 30–31.

18.11 Posters

Citation order:

- Artist (if known, or use title)
- Year (in round brackets)
- Title (in italics)
- [Poster]
- Exhibited at
- Location and date(s) of exhibition
- Dimensions (if relevant and available)

Example: poster copy of painting

In-text citation

The image (Chagall, no date) …

Reference list

Chagall, M. (no date) *Le violiniste* [Poster]. 84cm x 48cm/33" x 19".

Example: poster for exhibition

In-text citation

Smith's poster (2003) …

Reference list

Smith, K. (2003) *Prints, books and things* [Poster]. Exhibited at New York, Museum of Modern Art. 5 December 2003 to 8 March 2004.

18.12 Postcards

Citation order:

- Artist (if available)
- Year (in round brackets if available)
- Title (in italics)
- [Postcard]
- Place of publication: publisher

Example

In-text citation

The flat sandy beach (Corrance, no date) …

Reference list

Corrance, D. (no date) *Gairloch, Wester Ross* [Postcard]. Scotland: Stirling Gallery.

18.13 Maps

18.13 a. Ordnance Survey maps

Citation order:

- Ordnance Survey
- Year of publication (in round brackets)
- Title (in italics)
- Sheet number, scale
- Place of publication: publisher
- Series (in round brackets)

Example

In-text citation

Archaeological sites are italicised (Ordnance Survey, 2002).

Reference list

Ordnance Survey (2002) *Preston and Blackpool*, sheet 102, 1:50,000. Southampton: Ordnance Survey (Landranger series).

18.13 b. Geological Survey maps

Citation order:

- Corporate author and publisher
- Year of publication (in round brackets)
- Title (in italics)
- Sheet number, scale
- Place of publication: publisher
- Series (in round brackets)

Example

In-text citation

The landscape has undergone profound changes since the map (Ordnance Survey, 1980) was printed.

Reference list

Ordnance Survey (1980) *Bellingham (solid)*, sheet 13, 1:50,000. Southampton: Ordnance Survey. (Geological Survey of Great Britain [England and Wales]).

18.13 c. Online maps

Citation order:

- Map publisher
- Year of publication (in round brackets)
- Title of map section (in single quotation marks)

- Sheet number or tile, scale
- Available at: URL
- (Accessed: date)

Example

In-text citation

The leisure centre is close to Tiddenfoot Lake (Ordnance Survey, 2008).

Reference list

Ordnance Survey (2008) 'Tiddenfoot Lake', Tile sp92sw, 1:10,000. Available at: http://edina.ac.uk/digimap/ (Accessed: 3 May 2012).

Example

In-text citation

The dock layout and road network can be seen using *Google Maps* (Tele Atlas, 2012).

Reference list

Tele Atlas (2012) 'Cardiff Bay'. Available at: http://maps.google.co.uk (Accessed: 5 July 2012).

19. Live performances

19.1 Concerts

Citation order:
- Composer
- Year of performance (in round brackets)
- Title (in italics)
- Performed by … conducted by …
- Location. Date seen (in square brackets)

Example: classical concert

In-text citation

A wonderful premiere (Lord, 2007) …

Reference list

Lord, J. (2007) *Durham Concerto.* Performed by the Liverpool Philharmonic Orchestra conducted by Mischa Damev [Durham Cathedral, Durham. 20 October].

Example: band concert

In-text citation

The Kings of Leon (2008) wowed the crowd …

Reference list

Kings of Leon (2008) [Glastonbury Festival. 27 June].

19.2   Dance

Citation order:
- Composer or choreographer
- Year of premiere (in round brackets)
- Title (in italics)
- Location. Date seen (in square brackets)

Example

In-text citation

The performance was true to the intentions of its creator (Ashton, 1937).

Reference list

Ashton, F. (1937) *A wedding bouquet* [Royal Opera House, London. 22 October 2004].

19.3   Plays

Citation order:
- Title (in italics)
- by author
- Year of performance (in round brackets)
- Directed by
- Location. Date seen (in square brackets)

Example

In-text citation

One innovation was the use of Sellotape for the fairies' webs (*A midsummer night's dream*, 1995).

Reference list

A midsummer night's dream by William Shakespeare (1995) Directed by Ian Judge [Theatre Royal, Newcastle upon Tyne. 26 February].

20.   Audiovisual material

The internet has radically altered access to audio and visual sources and created the means for anyone to produce and distribute material. You may also view or hear programmes through catch-up services such as *BBC iPlayer*, *ITV Player*, *4 on Demand (4oD)*, *Demand 5* and *Sky Go* on a variety of devices. You do not need to specify the catch-up service nor the device. The nature of the material and the facts necessary to identify or retrieve it should dictate the substance of your in-text citations and reference list. Examples below will cite and reference traditional and online access routes.

20.1   Radio

20.1   a. Radio programmes

Citation order:
- Title of programme (in italics)
- Year of transmission (in round brackets)
- Name of channel
- Date of transmission (day/month)

Example

In-text citation

The latest report (*Today*, 2008) …

Reference list

Today (2008) BBC Radio 4, 15 August.

20.1   b. Radio programmes heard on the internet

You may listen to radio programmes live on the internet, or days after the original transmission through services such as the BBC's *iPlayer* and *Listen Again*. Specify the full date of the original broadcast as well as the date you accessed the programme.

Citation order:
- Title of programme (in italics)
- Year of original transmission (in round brackets)
- Name of channel
- Day and month of original transmission
- Available at: URL
- (Accessed: date)

Example

In-text citation

Technology offers the means to improve human ability (*Redesigning the human body*, 2006) …

Reference list

Redesigning the human body (2006) BBC Radio 4, 25 September. Available at: http://www.bbc.co.uk/radio4/redesigninghumanbody/ (Accessed: 15 June 2012).

20.2   Television

20.2   a. Television programmes

Citation order:
- Title of programme (in italics)
- Year of broadcast (in round brackets)
- Name of channel
- Broadcast date (day/month)

Example

In-text citation

The embarrassing corporate wannabes (*The Apprentice*, 2012) …

Reference list

The Apprentice (2012) BBC One Television, 23 June.

To quote something a character/presenter has said:

Example

In-text citation

'You're fired!' (Sugar, 2012) …

Reference list

Sugar, A. (2012) *The Apprentice*. BBC One Television, 23 June.

20.2 b. Episodes of a television series

Citation order:

- Title of episode (in single quotation marks)
- Year of broadcast (in round brackets)
- Title of programme (in italics)
- Series and episode numbers
- Name of channel
- Broadcast date (day/month)

Example

In-text citation

Some Daleks were mad and bad ('Asylum of the Daleks', 2012).

Reference list

'Asylum of the Daleks' (2012) *Doctor Who*, Series 33, episode 1. BBC One Television, 1 September.

20.2 c. Television programmes/ series on DVD/Blu-ray

Citation order:

- Title of episode (in single quotation marks)
- Year of distribution (in round brackets)
- Title of programme/series (in italics)
- Series and episode numbers (if known)
- Director and writer
- Date of original broadcast (if known)
- [DVD] or [Blu-ray]
- Place of distribution: distribution company

Example

In-text citation

The origins of the Doctor's most fearsome foe were revealed in 'Genesis of the Daleks' (2006).

Reference list

'Genesis of the Daleks' (2006) *Doctor Who*, episode 1. Directed by David Maloney. Written by Terry Nation. First broadcast 1975 [DVD]. London: BBC DVD.

20.2 d. Separate episodes from DVD/Blu-ray box-sets

Citation order:

- Title of episode (in single quotation marks)
- Year of distribution (in round brackets)
- Title of programme/series (in italics)
- 'In'
- Title of compilation or box-set (in italics)
- [DVD] or [Blu-ray]
- Place of distribution: distribution company

Example

In-text citation

Close attention was paid to period details, for example the costumes of the dancers ('Episode 4', 2006).

Reference list

'Episode 4' (2006) *The Mallen streak*. In *Catherine Cookson complete collection* [DVD]. London: ITV.

20.2 e. Television programmes viewed on the internet

Citation order:

- Title of episode (in single quotation marks) if known; if not, use title of programme
- Year of broadcast (in round brackets)
- Title of programme/series (in italics)
- Series and episode numbers (if known)
- Name of channel
- Broadcast date (day/month)
- Available at: URL
- (Accessed: date)

Example

In-text citation

The restoration of the lifeboat station was broadcast on *Grand Designs* ('Tenby', 2011).

Reference list

'Tenby' (2011) *Grand Designs*, Series 7, episode 30, Channel 4 Television, 28 September. Available at: http://www.channel4.com/programmes/grand-designs/episode-guide/series-7/episode-30 (Accessed: 15 January 2012).

20.3 Audio/video downloads

NB For audiobooks, see Section 1.3.

Music downloads are available from a range of different websites including *iTunes*, *Amazon*, *Spotify* and the band's or artist's website. When you have downloaded music onto an edevice, you may find it helpful to add a general statement at the end of your reference list informing your tutor that the track(s) is (are) available on your edevice.

Citation order:

- Author/singer/artist (if available; if not use title first)
- Year of distribution (in round brackets)
- Title of recording/video (in italics)
- Available at: URL
- (Downloaded: date)

Example

In-text citation

Their highly acclaimed album (The Civil Wars, 2012) …

Reference list

The Civil Wars (2012) *Barton Hollow*. Available at: http://www.myplaydirect.com/the-civil-wars (Downloaded: 5 August 2012).

20.4 Music or spoken word recordings on audio CDs or vinyl

If referring to *a single track, released on CD or vinyl as a single*, use the following citation order:

- Artist
- Year of distribution (in round brackets)
- Title of track (in italics)
- [CD] or [vinyl]
- Place of distribution: distribution company

Example

In-text citation

Her recent release (Jessie J, 2012) …

Reference list

Jessie J (2012) *Domino* [CD]. New York: Universal Republic Records.

If referring to *one track on a CD or vinyl album*, use the following citation order:

- Artist
- Year of distribution (in round brackets)
- Title of track (in single quotation marks)
- Title of album (in italics)
- [CD] or [vinyl]
- Place of distribution: distribution company

Example

In-text citation

Carpenter's song 'My heaven' (2004) …

Reference list

Carpenter, M.C. (2004) 'My heaven', *Between here and gone* [CD]. New York: Columbia Records.

If referencing *a whole album*, use the following citation order:

- Artist
- Year of distribution (in round brackets)
- Title of album (in italics)
- [CD] or [vinyl]
- Place of distribution: distribution company

Example

In-text citation

The band's acclaimed album (*Despite the snow*, 2008) …

Reference list

Emily Barker & The Red Clay Halo (2008) *Despite the snow* [CD]. London: Everyone Sang.

20.5 Music or spoken word recordings on audio cassettes

Citation order:

- Artist (if available; if not use title in italics first)
- Year of distribution (in round brackets)
- Title of recording (in italics)
- [Audio cassette]
- Place of publication: publisher

Example

In-text citation

Determination is a key attribute (*It's your choice: selection skills for managers*, 1993).

Reference list

It's your choice: selection skills for managers (1993) [Audio cassette]. London: Video Arts.

20.6 Liner notes

The liner notes in CD, DVD, vinyl and cassette containers often have information that can be referenced.

Citation order:

- Author
- Year (in round brackets)
- Title of liner notes text (in single quotation marks)
- 'in'
- Title of recording (in italics)
- [CD liner notes]
- Place of distribution: distribution company

Example

In-text citation

Thrills (1997, p. 11) described Weller's lyrics as 'sheer poetry'.

Reference list

Thrills, A. (1997) 'What a catalyst he turned out to be', in *The very best of The Jam* [CD liner notes]. London: Polydor.

20.7 Lyrics from songs/hymns

Citation order:

- Lyricist
- Year of distribution (in round brackets)
- Title of song/hymn (in italics)
- Place of distribution: distribution company

Example

In-text citation

Lennon and McCartney (1966) expressed the frustration of every new author:

'Dear Sir or Madam will you read my book?
It took me years to write, will you take a look?'

Reference list

Lennon, J. and McCartney, P. (1966) *Paperback writer*. Liverpool: Northern Songs Ltd.

20.8 Musical scores (sheet music)

Citation order:

- Composer
- Year of publication (in round brackets)
- Title of score (in italics)
- Notes
- Place of publication: publisher

Example

In-text citation

The composer's haunting evocation of the sea in *Fingal's Cave* (Mendelssohn, 1999) …

Reference list

Mendelssohn, F. (1999) *Fingal's Cave*. Edited from composer's notes by John Wilson. London: Initial Music Publishing.

20.9 Films/movies

20.9 a. Films/movies

Citation order:

- Title of film (in italics)
- Year of distribution (in round brackets)
- Directed by
- [Film]
- Place of distribution: distribution company

Example

In-text citation

Movies have been used to attack the President's policies (*Fahrenheit 9/11*, 2004).

Reference list

Fahrenheit 9/11 (2004) Directed by Michael Moore [Film]. Santa Monica, Calif: Lions Gate Films.

20.9   b. Films on DVD/Blu-ray

Citation order:

- Title of film (in italics)
- Year of distribution (in round brackets)
- Directed by
- [DVD] or [Blu-ray]
- Place of distribution: distribution company

> **Example**
>
> **In-text citation**
>
> Special effects can dominate a film, for example *The Matrix reloaded* (2003).
>
> **Reference list**
>
> *The Matrix reloaded* (2003) Directed by A. & L. Wachowski [DVD]. Los Angeles: Warner Brothers Inc.

Many films on DVD/Blu-ray come with additional material on other disks, such as interviews with actors and directors and outtakes. Here are examples for referencing some of this material.

20.9   c. Directors' commentaries on DVD/Blu-ray

Citation order:

- Name of commentator
- Year (in round brackets)
- Director's commentary (in single quotation marks)
- Name of film (in italics)
- Directed by
- [DVD] or [Blu-ray]
- Place of distribution: distribution company

> **Example**
>
> **In-text citation**
>
> The director thought this was a profitable franchise (Wachowski, 2003).
>
> **Reference list**
>
> Wachowski, A. (2003) 'Director's commentary', *The Matrix reloaded*. Directed by A. & L. Wachowski [DVD]. Los Angeles: Warner Brothers Inc.

20.9   d. Interviews with film directors

Citation order:

- Name of person interviewed
- Year of interview (in round brackets)
- Title of the interview (if any) (in single quotation marks)
- Interview with/interviewed by
- Interviewer's name
- Title of film (in italics)
- [DVD] or [Blu-ray]
- Place of distribution: distribution company

> **Example**
>
> **In-text citation**
>
> The director thought this was a profitable franchise (Wachowski, 2003).
>
> **Reference list**
>
> Wachowski, A. (2003) 'Interview with A. Wachowski'. Interviewed by L. Jones. *The Matrix reloaded* [DVD]. Los Angeles: Warner Brothers Inc.

20.9   e. Films on video cassettes

Citation order:

- Title of film or programme (in italics)
- Year of distribution (in round brackets)
- Directed by
- [Video cassette]
- Place of distribution: distribution company

Example

In-text citation

When the story finally made it to the silver screen (*The Lord of the Rings: the two towers*, 2003) …

Reference list

The Lord of the Rings: the two towers (2003) Directed by Peter Jackson [Video cassette]. New York: New Line Productions Inc.

20.9   f. Films on *YouTube*

Citation order:

- Name of person posting video
- Year video posted (in round brackets)
- Title of film or programme (in italics)
- Available at: URL
- (Accessed: date)

Example

In-text citation

The video (Leponline, 2008) …

Reference list

Leponline (2008) *Ask the experts – plastering a wall*. Available at: http://www.youtube.com/watch?v=J9wpcellxCU (Accessed: 13 January 2013).

20.10 Podcasts

Although podcasts can be downloaded onto portable devices, you should reference where it was published or displayed for download rather than trying to give 'my iPod' as a source.

Citation order:

- Author/presenter
- Year that the site was published/last updated (in round brackets)
- Title of podcast (in italics)
- [Podcast]
- Day/month of posted message
- Available at: URL
- (Accessed: date)

Example: with author/presenter

In-text citation

Verity *et al.* (2012) noted that the Olympics had a detrimental effect on sales.

Reference list

Verity, A., Laurie, D., Clark, M. and Naylor J. (2012) *Retail sales figures*. [Podcast]. 4 September. Available at: http://www.bbc.co.uk/podcasts/series/money (Accessed: 25 September 2012).

Example: without author

In-text citation

Internal networks are critical (Oracle Business Sense, 2013) …

Reference list

Oracle Business Sense (2013) *Structure* [Podcast]. 12 June. Available at: http://www.guardian.co.uk/podcast/0,,329509709,00.xml (Accessed: 27 June 2013).

20.11 Phonecasts

Phonecasts are audio or video programmes transmitted to a user's mobile phone. The user dials a number to access the programme. Alternatively, phonecasters can broadcast by using their telephones in place of microphones. Although phone calls are personal communications, it is possible to reference phonecasts if the access details are available in a publication or web page.

Citation order:

• Title of phonecast (in italics)
• Year of production (in round brackets)
• [Phonecast]
• Available at: URL
• (Accessed: date)

Example

In-text citation

Zuckerberg created *Facebook* in 2004 (*A conversation with Mark Zuckerberg*, 2007).

Reference list

A conversation with Mark Zuckerberg (2007) [Phonecast]. Available at: http://www.phonecasting.com/Channel/ViewChannel.aspx?id=1904 (Accessed: 11 July 2012).

20.12 Screencasts

Also called 'video screen captures', screencasts are digital recordings of computer screen activity. Screencast videos can provide instructions for using software applications.

Citation order:

• Title of screencast (in italics)
• Year of production (in round brackets)
• [Screencast]
• Available at: URL
• (Accessed: date)

Example

In-text citation

An online video demonstrated functions (*Learning Rails the zombie way*, no date).

Reference list

Learning Rails the zombie way (no date) [Screencast]. Available at: http://www.rubyonrails.org/screencasts (Accessed: 27 January 2013).

20.13 Vodcasts/vidcasts

Video podcasts can be viewed on the internet or downloaded for later viewing. So that readers can locate the original, cite and reference where you obtained the vodcast.

Citation order:

- Author
- Year that the site was published/last updated (in round brackets)
- Title of vodcast (in italics)
- [Vodcast]
- Available at: URL
- (Accessed: date)

Example

In-text citation

The vodcast (Walker and Carruthers, 2008) explained the proposal.

Reference list

Walker, A. and Carruthers, S. (2008) *Storage on your network* [Vodcast]. Available at: http://www.labrats.tv/episodes/ep126.html (Accessed: 19 June 2012).

20.14 Microform (microfiche and microfilm)

Citation order:

- Author
- Year of publication (in round brackets)
- Title of microform (in italics)
- Medium (in square brackets)
- Place of publication: publisher

Example

In-text citation

Data from Fritsch (1987) …

Reference list

Fritsch, F.E. (1987) *The Fritsch collection: algae illustrations on microfiche* [Microfiche]. Ambleside: Freshwater Biological Association.

21. Interviews

Citation order:

- Name of person interviewed
- Year of interview (in round brackets)
- Title of the interview (if any) (in single quotation marks)
- Interview with/interviewed by
- Interviewer's name
- Title of publication or broadcast (in italics)
- Day and month of interview, page numbers (if relevant)

Example: newspaper interview

In-text citation

Riley (2008) believed that 'imagination has to be captured by reality'.

Reference list

Riley, B. (2008) 'The life of Riley'. Interview with Bridget Riley. Interviewed by Jonathan Jones for *The Guardian*, 5 July, p. 33.

Example: television interview

In-text citation

The prime minister avoided the question (Blair, 2003).

Reference list

Blair, A. (2003) Interviewed by Jeremy Paxman for *Newsnight*, BBC Two Television, 2 February.

OR if published on the internet add:
- Available at: URL
- (Accessed: date)

Example: internet interview

In-text citation

The Democrat appeared confident in the discussion (Obama, 2008).

Reference list

Obama, B. (2008) Interviewed by Terry Moran for *ABC News*, 19 March. Available at: http://abcnews.go.com/Nightline/Vote2008/Story?id=4480133 (Accessed: 16 June 2008).

22.   Public communications

These include lectures, seminars, webinars, PowerPoint presentations, videoconferences/electronic discussion groups, bulletin boards/press releases, announcements/leaflets, advertisements/display boards, minutes of meetings and RSS feeds.

NB For communications in virtual learning environments, see Section 6.

22.1   Lectures/seminars/webinars/PowerPoint presentations/videoconferences

Citation order:
- Author/speaker
- Year (in round brackets)
- Title of communication (in italics)
- Medium (in square brackets)
- Module code: module title (in italics) (if known)
- Institution
- Day/month

Example

In-text citation

Points of interest from the lecture (Brown, 2012) …

Reference list

Brown, T. (2012) *Contemporary furniture* [Lecture to BSc Design Year 4], *DE816: Design for Industry*. Northumbria University. 21 April.

If referencing an *online communication*, use the following citation order:
- Author
- Year (in round brackets)
- Title of communication (in italics)
- Medium (in square brackets)
- Available at: URL
- (Accessed: date)

22.2 Electronic discussion groups and bulletin boards

NB For personal email correspondence, see Section 23.

The following examples deal with email correspondence made public in electronic conferences, discussion groups and bulletin boards.

Citation order:
- Author of message
- Year of message (in round brackets)
- Subject of the message (in single quotation marks)
- Discussion group or bulletin board (in italics)
- Date posted: day/month
- Available email: email address

22.3 Entire discussion groups or bulletin boards

Citation order:
- List name (in italics)
- Year of last update (in round brackets)
- Available email: email address
- (Accessed: date)

22.4 Press releases/ announcements

Citation order:
- Author/organisation
- Year issued (in round brackets)
- Title of communication (in italics)
- [Press release]
- Day/month

OR if available online, add:
- Available at: URL
- (Accessed: date)

> **Example**
>
> **In-text citation**
>
> This development (Google Inc., 2012) offered …
>
> **Reference list**
>
> Google Inc. (2012) *Google Maps heads north … way north* [Press release]. 23 August. Available at: http://www.google.com/intl/en/press/ (Accessed: 13 January 2013).

22.5   Leaflets

By their nature, leaflets are unlikely to have all the citation/reference elements, so include as much information as possible. It may also be useful to include a copy of a leaflet in an appendix to your assignment.

Citation order:
- Author (individual or corporate)
- Date (if available)
- Title (in italics)
- [Leaflet obtained …]
- Date obtained

> **Example**
>
> **In-text citation**
>
> Lloyds TSB Bank plc (no date) provides insurance for its mortgages.
>
> **Reference list**
>
> Lloyds TSB Bank plc (no date) *Mortgages*. [Leaflet obtained in Newcastle branch], 4 June 2013.

22.6   Advertisements

If referencing information in an advertisement, you will need to specify where it was seen. This might be online, in a newspaper, on television or in a location. Advertisements are often short-lived, so it is important to include the date you viewed them.

Citation order:
- Cite and reference according to the medium in which the advertisement appeared (see examples below)

> **Examples**
>
> **In-text citation**
>
> Advertisements by British Telecom (2012), Lloyds TSB (2013) and Northern Electric (2013) and that for the WOMAD festival in *The Guardian* (2013) …
>
> **Reference list**
>
> ### Example: television advertisement
>
> British Telecom (2012) *Office relocation gremlins* [Advertisement on ITV1 Television]. 23 November.
>
> ### Example: newspaper advertisement
>
> *The Guardian* (2013) 'WOMAD festival' [Advertisement]. 14 January, p. 12.
>
> ### Example: internet advertisement
>
> Lloyds TSB Bank plc (2013) *Selling your house?* [Advertisement]. Available at http://www.hotmail.com (Accessed: 13 February 2013).
>
> ### Example: billboard advertisement
>
> Northern Electric plc (2013) *Green energy* [Billboard at Ellison Road, Dunston-on-Tyne]. 14 January.

22.7 Display boards, for example in museums

It is very rare for an author to be given for information on display boards, so the example below uses the title first.

Citation order:
- Title (in italics)
- Year of production (if available)
- Display board at
- Name of venue, city
- Date observed

Example

In-text citation

Martin's vivid colours are a noted feature of his work (*Paintings of John Martin*, 2011).

Reference list

Paintings of John Martin (2011) Display board at Laing Art Gallery exhibition, Newcastle upon Tyne, 23 April 2013.

Example: with author identified

In-text citation

Jones (2013) suggested work shadowing and mentoring.

Reference list

Jones, T. (2013) 'Item 3.1: Developing our staff'. *Minutes of staff development committee meeting 23 February 2013*, Western Health Trust, Shrewsbury.

Example: with group name

In-text citation

The staff development committee (2013) suggested work shadowing and mentoring.

Reference list

Staff development committee (2013) 'Item 3.1: Developing our staff'. *Minutes of staff development committee meeting 23 February 2013*, Western Health Trust, Shrewsbury.

22.8 Minutes of meetings

Citation order:
- Author (individual or group if identified)
- Year of meeting (in round brackets)
- Item being referenced (in single quotation marks)
- Title and date of meeting (in italics)
- Organisation
- Location of meeting

22.9 RSS feeds

Really Simple Syndication (RSS) is a method of notifying subscribers if a favourite web page, for example a news source, has been updated. You should reference the details of the original source, for example news web page or newly published journal article, not the RSS feed.

Citation order:
- Author/organisation
- Year issued (in round brackets)
- Title of communication (in italics)
- [RSS]
- Day/month

OR if available online add:
- Available at: URL
- (Accessed: date)

Example

In-text citation

The library extension was completed in April 2012 (Durham University Library, 2012).

Reference list

Durham University Library (2012) *Library east wing opens* [RSS] 23 April. Available at: https://www.dur.ac.uk/feeds/news/?section=14. (Accessed: 25 April 2012).

---

23. Personal communications

NB For phonecasts, see Section 20.11.

Personal communications by face-to-face or telephone conversation, online methods such as Skype, letter, email, text message or fax can be referenced as follows.

Citation order:
- Sender/speaker/author
- Year of communication (in round brackets)
- Medium of communication
- Receiver of communication
- Day/month of communication

Examples

In-text citation

This was disputed by Walters (2012).

Reference list

Walters, F. (2012) Conversation with John Stephens, 13 August.

Walters, F. (2012) Letter to John Stephens, 23 January.

Walters, F. (2012) Email to John Stephens, 14 August.

Walters, F. (2012) Telephone conversation with John Stephens, 25 December.

Walters, F. (2012) Skype conversation with John Stephens, 21 June.

Walters, F. (2012) Text message to John Stephens, 14 June.

Walters, F. (2012) Fax to John Stephens, 17 December.

Note that both the in-text citations and references begin with the name of the sender of the communication.

NB You may need to seek permission from other parties in the correspondence before quoting them in your work. You might also include a copy of written communications in your appendices, or note where the communication/correspondence can be located (for example, library).

24. Genealogical sources

Use the name of the person(s) and the date of the event as the in-text citation and provide the full details in the reference list.

24.1 Birth, marriage and death certificates

Citation order:
- Name of person (in single quotation marks)
- Year of event (in round brackets)
- Certified copy of ... certificate for ... (in italics)
- Full name of person (forenames, surname) (in italics)
- Day/month/year of event (in italics)
- Application number from certificate
- Location of Register Office

OR if you retrieved the certificate online, after application number from certificate, add:
- Year of last update (in round brackets)
- Available at: URL
- (Accessed: date)

> **Example**
>
> **In-text citation**
>
> Amy was born in Bristol ('Amy Jane Bennett', 1874) ...
>
> **Reference list**
>
> 'Amy Jane Bennett' (1874) *Certified copy of birth certificate for Amy Jane Bennett, 10 April 1874*. Application number 4001788/C. Bristol Register Office.

24.2 Wills

Citation order:
- Title of document (in italics)
- Year of will (in round brackets)
- Name of archive or repository
- Reference number

> **Example**
>
> **In-text citation**
>
> Doubleday's nephews inherited his estates (*Will of Michael Doubleday of Alnwick Abbey, Northumberland*, 1797).
>
> **Reference list**
>
> *Will of Michael Doubleday of Alnwick Abbey, Northumberland* (1797) The National Archives: Public Record Office. Catalogue reference: PROB/11/1290.

24.3 Censuses

Citation order:
- Name of person (in single quotation marks)
- Year of census (in round brackets)
- Census return for ... (in italics)
- Street, place, county (in italics)
- Registration subdistrict (in italics)
- Public Record Office:
- Piece number, folio number, page number

OR if you retrieved the certificate online, add:
- Year of last update (in round brackets)
- Available at: URL
- (Accessed: date)

24.4 Parish registers

Citation order:

- Name of person (in single quotation marks)
- Year of event (in round brackets)
- Baptism, marriage or burial of …
- Full name of person (forenames, surname)
- Day/month/year of event
- Title of register (in italics)

OR if you retrieved the certificate online, add:

- Year of last update (in round brackets)
- Available at: URL
- (Accessed: date)

24.5 Military records

Citation order:

- Name of person (in single quotation marks)
- Year of publication (in round brackets)
- Title of publication (in italics)
- Publication details

OR if you retrieved the document online, add:

- Available at: URL
- (Accessed: date)

25. Manuscripts

If the author of a manuscript is known, use the following citation order:

- Author
- Year (in round brackets)
- Title of manuscript (in italics)
- Date (if available)
- Name of collection containing manuscript and reference number
- Location of manuscript in archive or repository

Example

In-text citation

The architect enjoyed a close relationship with his patron (Newton, 1785).

Reference list

Newton, W. (1785) *Letter to William Ord, 23 June*. Ord Manuscripts 324 E11/4, Northumberland Archives, Woodhorn.

Where the author of a manuscript is not known, use the following citation order:

- Title of manuscript (in italics)
- Year (if known, in round brackets)
- Name of collection containing manuscript and reference number
- Location of manuscript in archive or repository

Example

In-text citation

Expenditure was high in this period (*Fenham journal*, 1795).

Reference list

Fenham journal (1795) Ord Manuscripts, 324 E12, Northumberland Archives, Woodhorn.

To refer to a whole collection of manuscripts (MS), use the name of the collection.

Citation order:

- Location of collection in archive or repository
- Name of collection

Example

In-text citation

Consulting the family records (British Library, Lansdowne MS), the author discovered …

Reference list

British Library, Lansdowne MS.

Note that no date is given for a collection in the text or in the reference list as the collection contains items of various dates.

Section F.
American Psychological Association (APA) referencing style

The APA referencing style is used in some social science subjects. It uses an author-date format, like Harvard, to identify details in the text. Full details are given in an alphabetical list of references.

Conventions when using the APA referencing style

Multiple authors and et al.

- The APA insists that up to six authors are listed by name in an **in-text citation** and names are linked by '&' not 'and'.

> ### Example
> **In-text citation**
>
> Smith, Jones, Cassidy, Grey, Timms & Anders (2006) ... New research (Smith, Jones, Cassidy, Grey, Timms & Anders, 2006) ...

- If there are seven or more authors, use the first author and **et al**. for the in-text citation. Note that et al. is not italicized.

> ### Example
>
> Games can assist recovery (Weathers et al., 1981) ...

- But all authors should be listed in your **reference list**.

> ### Example
>
> Weathers, L., Bedell, J.R., Marlowe, H., Gordon, R.E., Adams, J., Reed, V., Palmer, J. & Gordon, K.K. (1981). Using psychotherapeutic games to train patients' skills. In R.E. Gordon and K.K. Gordon (Eds.) *Systems of treatment for the mentally ill* (pp. 109–124). New York: Grune & Stratton, 1981.

Year of publication

- In brackets, followed by a full stop.

Titles

- The titles of sources are italicised, as are volume numbers of journal articles, but not issue or page numbers
- Titles of articles within journals, or chapters within books, are not enclosed in quotation marks.

Capitalisation

- For a book title, only the first letter of the first word, the first letter of the first word of a subtitle and any **proper nouns** are capitalised.

> ### Example
>
> *Psychoanalysis: Its image and its public*

- For journal titles, each major word of the title is capitalised.

> ### Example
>
> *Journal of Comparative and Physiological Psychology*

Place of publication

For place of publication, you should always list the city and US state, using the two-letter abbreviation without full stops – for example, 'New York, NY'. Spell out the country names if outside the UK or the United States – for example 'Melbourne, Australia'.

Page numbers

- Page numbers for book chapters are given immediately after the title of the book in round brackets and before publication details.

Internet sources

- **Internet** sources should be indicated by Retrieved from **URL**, or **doi**:
  Note that APA style does not include a retrieval date for online sources
- APA also states that it is not necessary to include the name of the database when referencing online journals or ebook collections.

How to reference common sources

F.1 Books

Citation order:
- Author/editor
- Year of publication (in round brackets)
- Title (in italics)
- Edition (only include the edition number if it is not the first edition)
- Place of publication: publisher

> **Example**
>
> **In-text citation**
> Earlier analysis (Freud, 1936, p. 54) …
>
> **Reference list**
> Freud, A. (1936). *The ego and the mechanisms of defense*. New York, NY: International Universities Press.

F.2 Chapters/sections of edited books

Citation order:
- Author of the chapter/section (surname followed by initials)
- Year of publication (in round brackets)
- Title of chapter/section
- In
- Name of editor of book (Ed.)
- Title of book (in italics)
- Page numbers of chapter/section (in round brackets)
- Place of publication: publisher

> **Example**
>
> **In-text citation**
> The view proposed by Leites (1990, p. 444) …
>
> **Reference list**
> Leites, N. (1990). Transference interpretations only? In A.H. Esman (Ed.) *Essential papers on transference* (pp. 434–454). New York, NY: New York University Press.

F.3　Ebooks

Citation order:

- Author/editor
- Year of publication (in round brackets)
- Title (in italics)
- Retrieved from URL or doi:

> ### Example
> **In-text citation**
>
> More recent research (Lichtenberg, Lachmann & Fosshage, 2011, p. 54) …
>
> **Reference list**
>
> Lichtenberg, J.D., Lachmann, F.M. & Fosshage, J.L. (2011). *Psychoanalysis and motivational systems: a new look*. Retrieved from http://lib.myilibrary.com/ProductDetail.aspx?id=303727

F.4　Journal articles

Citation order:

- Author (surname followed by initials)
- Year of publication (in round brackets)
- Title of article
- Title of journal (in italics)
- Volume number (in italics)
- Issue (in round brackets): page numbers

> ### Example
> **In-text citation**
>
> Research by Frosch (2002) …
>
> **Reference list**
>
> Frosch, A. (2002). Transference: psychic reality and material reality. *Psychoanalytic Psychology*, *19*(4), 603–633.

F.5　Ejournal articles

Citation order:

- Author
- Year of publication (in round brackets)
- Title of article
- Title of journal (in italics)
- Volume number (in italics)
- Issue (in round brackets), page numbers
- Retrieved from URL or doi:

> ### Example
> **In-text citation**
>
> Violence is a factor in many instances of transference (Shubs, 2008).
>
> **Reference list**
>
> Shubs, C.H. (2008). Transference issues concerning victims of violent crime and other traumatic incidents of adulthood. *Psychoanalytic Psychology*, *25*(1), 122–141. doi: 10.1037/0736-9735.25.1.122

F.6　Organisation or personal internet sites

Citation order:

- Author
- Year the site was published/last updated (in round brackets)
- Title of internet site
- doi: or Retrieved from URL

Example

There are several career paths (British Psychological Association, 2012) …

British Psychological Association (2012). How to become a psychologist. Retrieved from http://www.bps.org.uk/careers-education-training/how-become-psychologist/how-become-psychologist

For **web pages** where no author can be identified, you should use the web page's title. If no title either, use the URL.

Example

As suggested by one website (Learn to profile people, 2008) …

Learn to profile people (2008). Retrieved from http://lifehacker.com/346372/learn-toprofile-people

Sample text

The theory of transference was developed by the research of Leites (1990) and Frosch (2002). Shubs (2008) has identified violence as a factor in transference.

Sample reference list

Frosch, A. (2002). Transference: psychic reality and material reality. *Psychoanalytic Psychology, 19*(4), 603–633.

Leites, N. (1990). Transference interpretations only? In A.H. Esman (ed.) *Essential papers on transference* (pp. 434–454). New York, NY: New York University Press.

Shubs, C.H. (2008). Transference issues concerning victims of violent crime and other traumatic incidents of adulthood. *Psychoanalytic Psychology, 25*(1), 122–141. doi: 10.1037/0736-9735.25.1.122

NB For more information on using the APA referencing style, see: American Psychological Association (2010) *Publication manual of the American Psychological Association*, 6th edn (Washington, DC: American Psychological Association).

Section G.
Modern Language Association (MLA) referencing style

The MLA referencing style is sometimes used in humanities subjects, including languages and literature. Emphasis is placed on the author's name (or if not available, the title of the source). The authors' full names, as written on the title pages, should be used. Sources are listed in a **Cited Works List** at the end of your work. Sources that are not cited in your text can be included in **footnotes** or **endnotes**. **In-text citations** use the author's name and if possible a page number within the source. To find the full details of the source being cited, the reader must refer to the Cited Works List.

Conventions when using the MLA referencing style

Author's name

- For in-text references and footnotes, give the author's name as forename(s) followed by surname, for example Peter Leach. For the Cited Works List, give surname, then forename(s), for example Leach, Peter.

Titles

- The titles of sources are italicised
- Capitalise the first word, all nouns, verbs and adjectives. Capitalise articles if they are the first words of a subtitle after a colon, for example *Cite Them Right: The Essential Referencing Guide*.

Page numbers

- Do not use p. or pp. Page numbers of chapters and articles are elided, for example 127–45.

Web addresses

- A major revision of MLA advice on referencing online sources occurred with the 7th edition of the *MLA Handbook for Writers of Research Papers*. New York: Modern Language Association of America, 2009. Previous editions included the **URL** of a website at the end of the reference. However, the MLA assumes that most readers will be able to locate an online source using a search engine. Therefore, the MLA advises that you do not include URLs in your references and instead use the word Web, followed by the date (see Section G.5). Only if you think that a reader will be unable to locate a source using a search engine should you include the URL in angle brackets, for example <URL> after the date of access (see Section G.6).

Footnotes or endnotes

- You can use footnotes or endnotes in the MLA referencing style to bring in additional information. Use a **superscript number** for the footnote.

How to cite common sources in your text

You can phrase your text to note the author's view.

Or you can cite the author and page number after the section of their work you have referred to.

Note that there is no comma between the author and the page number and that there is no p. before the page number. If there is no author, use the title of the source and the page number.

Sample text

The following sample piece of text shows how various sources would be included as in-text citations:

Worsley (*Classical Architecture*) highlighted the variety of styles that eighteenth-century architects employed in their buildings. Initially British architects relied upon the designs of Andrea Palladio, a sixteenth-century Italian architect, who was believed to have studied ancient Roman buildings (*Palladio's Italian Villas*). As the century progressed, however, more authentic Roman examples were studied, particularly after the discovery of Pompeii (Nappo). Rich patrons wanted designs in the latest fashion and among those to profit from this demand was Robert Adam, who published his studies of Roman buildings (Adam). With this first-hand knowledge he designed many country houses and public buildings. His work was not always as revolutionary as he claimed (Worsley 265), but it certainly impressed clients. Peter Leach noted that Adam was even able to take over projects begun by other architects, as at Kedleston in Derbyshire (159). Although most patrons favoured classical styles, Horace Walpole suggested that the Gothic style was 'our architecture', the national style of England (Walpole, cited in Lang 251). Alexandrina Buchanan suggested that Gothic style signified ancient lineage and the British Constitution (43).

How to reference common sources in the Cited Works List

G.1 Books

Citation order:
- Author/editor (surname, forename)
- Title (in italics)
- Edition (only include the edition number if it is not the first edition)
- Place of publication: publisher
- Year of publication
- Medium of publication

G.2   Ebooks

Citation order:

- Author/editor (surname, forename)
- Title (in italics)
- Edition (only include the edition number if it is not the first edition)
- Place of publication: publisher
- Year of publication
- Source of ebook (in italics)
- Web
- Date of access

Example

Cited Works List

Soane, John. *Designs in Architecture, Consisting of Plans, Elevations, and Sections, for Temples, Baths, Cassines, Pavilions, Garden-Seats, Obelisks, and Other Buildings; for Decorating Pleasure Grounds, Parks, Forests*. London: printed for I. & J. Taylor, 1790. *Eighteenth Century Collections Online*. Web. 21 August 2012.

G.3   Chapters/sections of edited books

Citation order:

- Author of the chapter/section (surname, forename)
- Title of chapter/section (in double quotation marks)
- Title of book (in italics)
- Ed. and name of editor of book
- Place of publication: publisher
- Year of publication
- Page numbers of chapter/section

Example

Cited Works List

Buchanan, Alexandrina. "Interpretations of Medieval Architecture." *Gothic Architecture and Its Meanings 1550–1830*. Ed. Michael Hall. Reading: Spire Books, 2002. 27–52.

G.4   Journal articles

Citation order:

- Author (surname, forename)
- Title of article (in double quotation marks)
- Title of journal (in italics)
- Volume number. Issue number
- Year of publication (in round brackets) followed by colon
- Page numbers of journal article

Example

Cited Works List

Leach, Peter. "James Paine's Design for the South Front of Kedleston Hall: Dating and Sources." *Architectural History* 40 (1997): 159–70.

G.5   Ejournal articles

Citation order:

- Author (surname, forename or initial)
- Title of article (in double quotation marks)
- Title of journal (in italics)
- Volume number. Issue number
- Year (in round brackets) followed by colon
- Page numbers of article
- Name of collection (in italics)
- Web
- Date of access

Example

Lang, S. "The Principles of the Gothic Revival in England." *Journal of the Society of Architectural Historians* 25.4 (1966): 240–67. *JSTOR*. Web. 21 August 2012.

G.6 Organisation or personal internet sites

Citation order:

- Author (surname, forename)
- Title of internet site (in italics)
- Year that the site was published/last updated
- Web
- Date of access
- <URL> (if included)

Example

Nappo, Salvatore. *Pompeii: Its Discovery and Preservation*. 2012. Web. 21 August 2012. <http://www.bbc.co.uk/history/ancient/romans/pompeii_rediscovery_01.shtml>.

For **web pages** where no author can be identified, you should use the web page's title.

Example

Palladio's Italian Villas. 2005. Web. 21 August 2012. <http://www.boglewood.com/palladio/>.

Sample Cited Works List

All sources are listed alphabetically in the Cited Works List, giving all details of author, title and publication. In keeping with the emphasis upon authors' names, the first line of the reference is not indented, but subsequent lines are, so that authors' names are easily identifiable. The Cited Works List for the sample text on page 89 would look like this:

Adam, Robert. *Ruins of the Palace of the Emperor Diocletian at Spalatro in Dalmatia*. London, 1764. *Eighteenth Century Collections Online*. Web. 21 August 2012.

Buchanan, Alexandrina. "Interpretations of Medieval Architecture." *Gothic Architecture and Its Meanings 1550–1830*. Ed. Michael Hall. Reading: Spire Books, 2002, 27–52.

Lang, S. "The Principles of the Gothic Revival in England." *Journal of the Society of Architectural Historians* 25.4 (1966): 240–67, *JSTOR*. Web. 21 August 2012.

Leach, Peter. "James Paine's Design for the South Front of Kedleston Hall: Dating and Sources." *Architectural History* 40 (1997): 159–70.

Nappo, Salvatore. *Pompeii: Its Discovery and Preservation*. 2012. Web. 21 August 2012. <http://www.bbc.co.uk/history/ancient/romans/pompeii_rediscovery_01.shtml>.

Palladio's Italian Villas. 2005. Web. 21 August 2012. <http://www.boglewood.com/palladio/>.

Worsley, Giles. *Classical Architecture in Britain: The Heroic Age*. London: Published for the Paul Mellon Centre for Studies in British Art by Yale University Press, 1995.

NB For more information on using the MLA referencing style, see Modern Language Association (2009) *MLA Handbook for Writers of Research Papers*. 7th edn. New York: Modern Language Association of America.

Section H.
Modern Humanities Research Association (MHRA) referencing style

The MHRA referencing style is used in some arts and humanities publications. It uses a numeric style.

Citing sources in your text

Instead of naming authors in the text, which can be distracting for the reader, numbers are used to denote **citations**. These numbers in the text are linked to a full **reference** in **footnotes** or **endnotes** and in your **bibliography**. Word processing software such as Microsoft Word can create this link between citation number and full reference.

Cited publications are numbered in the order in which they are first referred to in the text. They are usually identified by a **superscript number**, for example Thomas corrected this error.[1]

If the citation is not shown by a superscript number, it might be in round brackets, for example, Thomas corrected this error. (1)

Or it might be in square brackets, for example, Thomas corrected this error. [1]

Conventions when using the MHRA referencing style

Footnotes and endnotes

* The use of modern word processing software has led to a resurgence in the use of footnotes or endnotes. These can be used in MHRA referencing style to keep bibliographic details out of the flow of text, and can also be used to add additional information that may not fit easily into the main body of your work. Check whether footnotes or endnotes are preferred for the work you are producing.

First citation and subsequent short citations

* Note that the first time you cite a source, you should give full details in the footnote or endnote. Subsequent entries to the same source can be abbreviated to author's surname and the first few words of the title, plus a page number if you are citing a specific part of the text, giving you a **short citation**, for example:

Worsley, *Classical Architecture*, p. 25.

The sample text at the end of this section shows examples of a first citation and subsequent short citation of this book by Worsley.

* Note that the use of short citations, which are more precise, replaces **op. cit.**

* As well as footnotes or endnotes, you should list all your sources, including those you have read but not cited, in a bibliography at the end of your work.

ibid.

* *ibid.* (from Latin, *ibidem*) means 'in the same place'. If two (or more) consecutive references are from the same source, then the second (or others) is cited *ibid.*, for example:
  1. Paul Gester, *Finding Information on the Internet* (London: John Wiley, 1999), pp. 133–81.
  2. *ibid.*, p. 155.
  3. *ibid.*, p. 170.

Capitalisation

- Capitalise the first letter of the first word, all nouns, verbs and adjectives. Also capitalise articles if they are the first words of a subtitle after a colon, for example *Cite Them Right: The Essential Referencing Guide*.

Internet addresses (URLs)

- The **internet** address is given in full, but with < in front and > after the address, for example <http://news.bbc.co.uk> then [accessed date].

Author names

- Note that in the footnotes, author names should be forename followed by surname, for example Francis Wheen. In the bibliography, author names should be surname followed by forename, for example Wheen, Francis.

Commas

- Use commas to separate the elements of the reference.

Page numbers

- Use p. or pp. for books but not for journal articles.

How to reference common sources in your bibliography

H.1 Books

Citation order:
- Author/editor
- Title (in italics)
- Edition (only include the edition number if it is not the first edition)
- Place of publication: publisher, year of publication (all in round brackets)

Example

Bibliography

Worsley, Giles, *Classical Architecture in Britain: The Heroic Age* (London: Published for the Paul Mellon Centre for Studies in British Art by Yale University Press, 1995).

H.2 Ebooks

Citation order:
- Author/editor
- Title (in italics)
- Edition (only include the edition number if it is not the first edition)
- Place of publication: publisher, year of publication (all in round brackets)
- In
- Title of online collection (in italics)
- <URL of collection>
- [accessed date]

Example

Bibliography

Adam, Robert, *Ruins of the Palace of the Emperor Diocletian at Spalatro in Dalmatia* (London: Printed for the author, 1764), in *Eighteenth Century Collections Online*, <http://galenet.galegroup.com/servlet/ECCO> [accessed 21 August 2012].

H.3 Chapters/sections of edited books

Citation order:
- Author of the chapter/section
- Title of chapter/section (in single quotation marks)
- in

- Title of book (in italics)
- ed. by
- Name of editor of book
- Place of publication: publisher, year of publication (all in round brackets)
- Page numbers of chapter/section (preceded by pp.)

> **Example**
>
> Bibliography
>
> Buchanan, Alexandrina, 'Interpretations of Medieval Architecture', in *Gothic Architecture and Its Meanings 1550–1830*, ed. by Michael Hall (Reading: Spire Books, 2002), pp. 27–52.

H.4 Journal articles

Citation order:
- Author
- Title of article (in single quotation marks)
- Title of journal (in italics and capitalise first letter of each word in title, except for linking words such as and, of, the, for)
- Volume number. Issue number
- Year of publication (in round brackets)
- Page numbers of article (not preceded by pp.)

> **Example**
>
> Bibliography
>
> Leach, Peter, 'James Paine's Design for the South Front of Kedleston Hall: Dating and Sources', *Architectural History*, 40 (1997),159–70.

H.5 Ejournal articles

Citation order:
- Author

- Title of article (in single quotation marks)
- Title of journal (in italics and capitalise first letter of each word in title, except for linking words such as and, of, the, for)
- Volume number. Issue number yes
- Year of publication (in round brackets)
- Page numbers of article
- in
- Name of collection (in italics)
- <URL> or <DOI>
- [accessed date]

> **Example**
>
> Bibliography
>
> Lang, S., 'The Principles of the Gothic Revival in England', *Journal of the Society of Architectural Historians*, 25.4 (1966), 240–67, in *JSTOR*, <http://www.jstor.org/stable/988353> [accessed 21 August 2012].

H.6 Organisation or personal internet sites

Citation order:
- Author
- Title of internet site (in italics)
- Year that the site was published/last updated (in round brackets)
- <URL>
- [accessed date]

> **Example**
>
> Bibliography
>
> Nappo, Salvatore Ciro, *Pompeii: Its Discovery and Preservation* (2012), <http://www.bbc.co.uk/history/ancient/romans/pompeii_rediscovery_01.shtml> [accessed 21 August 2012].

For **web pages** where no author can be identified, you should use the web page's title. If no title either, use the **URL**.

H.7 Manuscripts in archives

Citation order:
- Place
- Name of archive
- Reference number
- Description of document

Sample text

This sample piece of text shows how various sources would be included as in-text citations:

Worsley's *Classical Architecture* highlighted the variety of styles that eighteenth-century architects employed in their buildings.[1] Initially British architects relied upon the designs of Andrea Palladio, a sixteenth-century Italian architect, who was believed to have studied ancient Roman buildings.[2] As the century progressed, however, more authentic Roman examples were studied, particularly after the discovery of Pompeii.[3]

Rich patrons wanted designs in the latest fashion and among those to profit from this demand was Robert Adam, who published his studies of Roman buildings.[4] With this first-hand knowledge he designed many country houses and public buildings.[5] His work was not always as revolutionary as he claimed,[6] but it certainly impressed clients. Adam was even able to take over projects begun by other architects, as at Kedleston in Derbyshire.[7]

Although most patrons favoured classical styles, Horace Walpole suggested that the Gothic style was 'our architecture', the national style of England.[8] Later authors have suggested that Gothic style signified ancient lineage and the British Constitution.[9]

Sample footnotes

1. Giles Worsley, *Classical Architecture in Britain: The Heroic Age* (London: Published for the Paul Mellon Centre for Studies in British Art by Yale University Press, 1995).

2. *Palladio's Italian Villas* (2005), <http://www.boglewood.com/palladio/> [accessed 2 June 2008].

3. Salvatore Ciro Nappo, *Pompeii: Its Discovery and Preservation* (2012), http://www.bbc.co.uk/history/ancient/romans/pompeii_rediscovery_01.shtml [accessed 21 August 2012].

4. Robert Adam, *Ruins of the Palace of the Emperor Diocletian at Spalatro in Dalmatia* (London: Printed for the author, 1764), in *Eighteenth Century Collections Online*, <http://galenet.galegroup.com/servlet/ECCO> [accessed 21 August 2012].

5. *Treasures of Britain and Treasures of Ireland* (London: Reader's Digest Association Ltd, 1990).

6. Worsley, *Classical Architecture*, p. 265.

7. Peter Leach, 'James Paine's Design for the South Front of Kedleston Hall: Dating and Sources', *Architectural History*, 40 (1997),159–70.

8. Horace Walpole, cited in S. Lang, 'The Principles of the Gothic Revival in England', *Journal of the Society of Architectural Historians*, 25.4 (1966), 240–67, in *JSTOR*, <http://www.jstor.org/stable/988353> [accessed 21 August 2012].

9. Alexandrina Buchanan, 'Interpretations of Medieval Architecture', in *Gothic Architecture and Its Meanings 1550–1830*, ed. by Michael Hall (Reading: Spire Books, 2002), pp. 27–52.

NB Footnote 6 is an example of a short citation, and footnote 8 is a secondary reference.

Sample bibliography

The bibliography should include sources you have cited in footnotes and any sources you have read but not cited directly. In the bibliography, the authors' names should appear in alphabetical order by surname. The bibliography for the works cited in the sample text above would look like this:

Adam, Robert, *Ruins of the Palace of the Emperor Diocletian at Spalatro in Dalmatia* (London: Printed for the author, 1764), in *Eighteenth Century Collections Online*, <http://galenet.galegroup.com/servlet/ECCO> [accessed 21 August 2012].

Buchanan, Alexandrina, 'Interpretations of Medieval Architecture', in *Gothic Architecture and Its Meanings 1550–1830*, ed. by Michael Hall (Reading: Spire Books, 2002), pp. 27–52.

Lang, S., 'The Principles of the Gothic Revival in England', *Journal of the Society of Architectural Historians*, 25.4 (1966), 240–67, in *JSTOR*, <http://www.jstor.org/stable/988353> [accessed 21 August 2012].

Leach, Peter, 'James Paine's Design for the South Front of Kedleston Hall: Dating and Sources', *Architectural History*, 40 (1997),159–70.

Nappo, Salvatore Ciro, *Pompeii: Its Discovery and Preservation* (2012), <http://www.bbc.co.uk/history/ancient/romans/pompeii_rediscovery_01.shtml> [accessed 21 August 2012].

Palladio's Italian Villas (2005), <http://www.boglewood.com/palladio/> [accessed 21 August 2012].

Treasures of Britain and Treasures of Ireland (London: Reader's Digest Association Ltd, 1990).

Worsley, Giles, *Classical Architecture in Britain: The Heroic Age*. (London: Published for the Paul Mellon Centre for Studies in British Art by Yale University Press, 1995).

NB For more information on using the MHRA referencing style, see http://www.mhra.org.uk/Publications/Books/StyleGuide/download.shtml.

Section I.
Oxford University Standard for the Citation of Legal Authorities (OSCOLA)

There are established guidelines for the referencing of legal materials. Many UK law schools and legal publications use the 4th edition of the Oxford University Standard for the Citation of Legal Authorities (OSCOLA); examples of referencing common legal sources in the OSCOLA format are given below.

Conventions when using the OSCOLA referencing style

- OSCOLA uses numeric references in the text linked to full **citations** in **footnotes**
- Very little punctuation is used
- Well-established abbreviations are used for legal sources such as law reports and parliamentary publications. For details of the accepted abbreviations for legal publications, see the Cardiff University *Cardiff Index to Legal Abbreviations* at http://www.legalabbrevs.cardiff.ac.uk/
- OSCOLA assumes that you are referencing UK legal sources. If you are writing about legal material in several countries, use abbreviations of the nations to denote different jurisdictions, for example Access to Justice Act 1999 (UK); Homeland Security Act 2001 (USA).

Pinpointing

If you wish to cite a specific page within a source, include this page number at the end of the reference. For example, if you wished to pinpoint something on page 1357 of a report running from pages 1354–1372, you would write:

R v Dunlop [2006] EWCA Crim 1354, 1357

How to reference common sources

I.1   Books

Citation order:
- Author,
- Book title (in italics and capitalise first letter of each word in title, except for linking words such as and, or, the, for)
- (Edition, Publisher year)

> **Example in footnotes**
>
> CMV Clarkson, *Criminal Law: Text and Materials* (7th edn, Sweet & Maxwell 2010)

I.2   Chapters in edited books

Citation order:
- Author,
- 'Chapter title'
- in editor (ed),
- Book title (in italics)
- (Edition, Publisher year)

> **Example in footnotes**
>
> Paul Matthews, 'The Legal and Moral Limits of Common Law Tracing' in Peter Birks (ed), *Laundering and Tracing* (Clarendon Press 1995)

I.3 Journal articles

Citation order:
- Author,
- Article title (in single quotation marks)
- Year (use square brackets if it identifies the volume, use round brackets if there is a separate volume number)
- Volume number
- Abbreviated journal title,
- First page number

> **Example in footnotes: with volume number**
>
> AJ Roberts, 'Evidence: Bad Character – Pre-Criminal Justice Act 2003 Law' (2008) 4 Crim LR, 303

> **Example in footnotes: with no volume number**
>
> Po-Jen Yap, 'Defending Dialogue' [2012] PL 527

I.4 Ejournal articles

Citation order:
- Author
- Article title (in single quotation marks)
- [Year] or (Year)
- Volume number
- Abbreviated journal title
- First page number
- <URL> or <doi>
- accessed date

> **Example in footnotes**
>
> Cormac Behan and Ian O'Donnell, 'Prisoners, Politics and the Polls: Enfranchisement and the Burden of Responsibility' (2008) 48(3) Brit J Criminol, 31 <doi:10.1093/bjc/azn004> accessed 29 July 2012

I.5 Bills (House of Commons and House of Lords)

Citation order:
- Short title
- House in which it originated
- Parliamentary session (in round brackets)
- Bill number (in square brackets for Commons Bills, no brackets for Lords Bills)

> **Examples in footnotes**
>
> Transport HC Bill (1999–2000) [8]
>
> Transport HL Bill (2007–08) 1

I.6 UK statutes (Acts of Parliament)

A major change in the citation of UK legal sources took place in 1963. Before this, an Act was cited according to the regnal year (that is, the number of years since the monarch's accession).

I.6 a. Pre-1963 statutes

Citation order:
- Title of Act and year
- Regnal year
- Name of sovereign
- Chapter number

I.6 b. Post-1963 statutes

Use the short title of an Act, with the year in which it was enacted.

Citation order:
- Short title of Act
- Year enacted

Example in footnotes

Access to Justice Act 1999

I.6 c. Parts of Acts

Citation order:
- Short title of Act
- Year enacted
- Pt for Part
- s for section number
- Subsection number (in round brackets)
- Paragraph number (in round brackets)

Example in footnotes

Finance Act 2007, Pt1, s 2(1)(b)

I.7 Statutory Instruments (SIs)

Citation order:
- Name/title
- SI year/number

Example in footnotes

Terrorism (United Nations Measures) Order 2001, SI 2001/3365

I.8 Command Papers

Citation order:
- Author
- Title (in italics)
- Paper number and year (in round brackets)

Example in footnotes

Lord Chancellor's Department, *Government Policy on Archives* (Cm 4516, 1999)

I.9 Law reports (cases)

Citation order:
- Name of parties involved in case (in italics)
- Year (use square brackets if the year identifies the volume, use round brackets if each annual volume is numbered and the year is not required to identify the volume)
- Volume number and abbreviation for name of report and first page of report

Example in footnotes: with [Year]

Hazell v Hammersmith and Fulham London Borough Council [1992] 2 AC 1

NB Date in square brackets because the year identifies the volume required. In this instance, the 2 means that this case appeared in the second volume for the year 1992.

Example in footnotes: with (Year)

R v Edwards (John) (1991) 93 Cr App R 48

NB Date in round brackets because there is also a volume number, this is the 93rd volume of Criminal Appeal Reports.

Neutral citations

From 2002 cases have been given a neutral citation that identifies the case without referring to the printed law report series in which the case was published. This helps to identify the case online, for example through the freely available transcripts of the British and Irish Legal Information Institute (www.bailii.org).

Citation order:
- Name of parties involved in case (in italics)
- [Year]
- Court
- Number of case in that year

> **Example in footnotes**
>
> *Humphreys v Revenue and Customs* [2012] UKSC 18

This shows that Humphreys v Revenue and Customs was the 18th case heard by the United Kingdom Supreme Court in 2012.

The use of neutral citations does not help with locating cases in printed law reports. You will need to add the citation for the law report after the neutral citation.

> **Example in footnotes**
>
> *Humphreys v Revenue and Customs* [2012] UKSC 18, [2012] 1 WLR 1545

This shows that the case was reported in the first volume of the Weekly Law Reports for 2012, starting on page 1545.

Citing names of judges

If you wish to quote something said by a judge, include their name in your text associated with the source you are citing:

In *R v Jones*,[7] Williams LJ noted …

If the judge is a peer, you would write, for example, 'Lord Blackstone'. If the judge is a Mr, Mrs or Ms, you would write 'Blackstone J' (J for judge); if a Lord Justice or Lady Justice, you would write 'Blackstone LJ'.

> **Example in footnotes**
>
> 7. *R v Jones* [2009] EWCA Crim 120

I.10   Hansard

Hansard is the official record of debates and speeches given in Parliament.

Citation order:
- Abbreviation of House
- Deb (for Debates)
- Date of debate
- Volume number
- Column number

> **Examples in footnotes**
>
> HC Deb 19 June 2008, vol 477, col 1183
>
> - If you are citing a Commons Written Answer, use the suffix W after the column number, for example
>
> HC Deb 19 June 2008, vol 477, col 1106W

- If you are citing a Lords Written Answer, use the prefix WA before the column number, for example

HL Deb 19 June 2008, vol 702, col WA200

- Use the suffix WS if you are citing a Written Statement, for example

HC Deb 18 September 2006, vol 449, col 134WS

- Use the suffix WH if you are citing a debate in Westminster Hall, for example

HC Deb 21 May 2008, vol 476, col 101WH

- If quoting very old Hansards, it is usual, although optional, to include the series number:

HC Deb (5th series) 13 January 1907 vol 878, cols 69–70

- In 2007, the earlier system of Standing Committees was replaced by Public Bill Committees. Standing Committee Hansard should be cited as follows:

SC Deb (A) 13 May 1998, col 345

The new Public Bill Committees would be cited thus:

Health Bill Deb 30 January 2007, cols 12–15

unless the Bill title is so long that this becomes ridiculous. In this case use:

PBC Deb (Bill 99) 30 January 2007, cols 12–15

or, where the context makes the Bill obvious:

PBC Deb 30 January 2007, cols 12–15

For more information on the use of Hansard, see *Factsheet G17: The Official Report* (2010) produced by the House of Commons Information Office. Available at: http://www.parliament.uk/documents/upload/g17.pdf (Accessed: 29 July 2012).

A fully searchable version of Hansard from 1988 for the Commons and from 1995 for the Lords is available online at http://www.parliament.uk/business/publications/hansard/ (Accessed: 29 July 2012).

I.11 Legislation from devolved Assemblies

I.11 a. Acts of the Scottish Parliament

For Acts of the post-devolution Scottish Parliament, replace the Chapter number with 'asp' (meaning Act of the Scottish Parliament).

Citation order:
- Title of Act including year
- (asp number)

Example in footnotes

Budget (Scotland) Act 2004 (asp 2)

I.11 b. Scottish Statutory Instruments (SSIs)

Citation order:
- Title including year,
- SSI number

Example

Reference list

Tuberculosis (Scotland) Order 2005, SSI 2005/434

I.11   c. Acts of the Northern Ireland Assembly

Citation order:
- Title of Act (Northern Ireland)
- Year

> **Example**
>
>
> Ground Rents Act (Northern Ireland) 2001

I.11   d. Statutory Rules of Northern Ireland

The Northern Ireland Assembly may pass Statutory Instruments. These are called Statutory Rules of Northern Ireland.

Citation order:
- Title of Rule (Northern Ireland)
- Year
- SR year/number

> **Example in footnotes**
>
> Smoke Flavourings Regulations (Northern Ireland) 2005, SR 2005/76

I.11   e. National Assembly for Wales legislation

The National Assembly for Wales may pass Assembly Measures (nawm), which are primary legislation but are subordinate to UK statutes.

Citation order:
- Title of Assembly Measure
- Year
- (nawm number)

> **Example in footnotes**
>
> NHS Redress (Wales) Measure 2008 (nawm 1)

The National Assembly for Wales may also pass Statutory Instruments. As well as the SI number and year, Welsh Statutory Instruments have a W. number.

Citation order:
- Title of Order (Wales)
- Year
- Year/SI number (W. number)

> **Example in footnotes**
>
> The Bluetongue (Wales) Order 2003 Welsh Statutory Instrument 2003/326 (W. 47)

I.12   Law Commission reports and consultation papers

Citation order:
- Law Commission
- Title of report or consultation paper (in italics)
- Number of report or consultation paper, Command Paper number (if given) (in round brackets)
- Page number of cited text

> **Example in footnotes**
>
> Law Commission, *Double Jeopardy and Prosecution Appeals* (Law Com No 267, 2001)

I.13　European Union (EU) legal sources

EU legislation may be legislation, directives, decisions and regulations.

I.13　a. EU legislation

Citation order:

- Legislation title
- Year (in square brackets)
- Official Journal (OJ) series
- Issue/first page

Example in footnotes

Consolidated Version of the Treaty on European Union [2008] OJ C 115/13

I. 13　b. EU directives, decisions and regulations

Citation order:

- Legislation type
- Number and title
- Year (in square brackets)
- Official Journal (OJ) L series
- Issue/first page

Example in footnotes

Council Directive 2008/52/EC on certain aspects of mediation in civil and commercial matters [2008] OJ L 136/3

I.14　United Nations documents

Citation order:

- Author
- Title
- Date
- Document number

Example in footnotes

UNSC Res 1970 (26 February 2011) UN Doc S/RES/1970

I.15　United States legal material

For information on citing and referencing US legal material, see *The bluebook: a uniform system of citation* (2005) Harvard Law Review Association. A useful online guide is Martin, P.W. (2011) *Introduction to basic legal citation*. Available at: http://www.law.cornell.edu/citation/ (Accessed: 11 August 2012).

Sample text

The judge noted the case of *R v Edwards*.[1] The Access to Justice Act 1999[2] and the Terrorism (United Nations Measures) Order[3] strengthened this interpretation. An alternative view was suggested by Clarkson[4] and most recently by Behan and O'Donnell.[5] They have questioned the exclusion of evidence in the case.[6]

Sample footnotes

1. *R v Edwards (John)* (1991) 93 Cr App R 48

2. Access to Justice Act 1999

3. Terrorism (United Nations Measures) Order 2001, SI 2001/3365

4. CMV Clarkson, *Criminal Law: Text and Materials* (7th edn, Sweet & Maxwell 2010)

5. Cormac Behan and Ian O'Donnell, 'Prisoners, Politics and the Polls: Enfranchisement and the Burden of

Responsibility' (2008) 48(3) Brit J Criminol, 31 <doi:10.1093/bjc/azn004> accessed 29 July 2012

6. *R v Edwards* (n1) 53

NB Footnote 6 refers the reader back to footnote 1 (n1) where the full reference is given, but directs attention to what is written on page 53.

Bibliographies

OSCOLA (2012, 4th edn) suggests that for longer assignments such as theses, and for books, a separate **bibliography** listing secondary sources (everything except legislation and cases) should be provided. Some law schools require that students provide a separate bibliography with all assignments, so check with your tutor if a bibliography is required as well as footnotes.

Authors' names should have surname, then initials of given names (not full given names).This should be in alphabetical order by authors' name. Any works without an author should start with a dash, followed by the title. These unattributed sources are listed at the beginning of the bibliography in alphabetical order by the first major word of the title. A sample bibliography for the examples of secondary sources in this section is shown below:

Behan C and O'Donnell I, 'Prisoners, Politics and the Polls: Enfranchisement and the Burden of Responsibility' (2008) 48(3) Brit J Criminol, 31 <doi:10.1093/bjc/azn004> accessed 29 July 2012

Clarkson CMV, *Criminal Law: Text and Materials* (7th edn, Sweet & Maxwell 2010)

Law Commission, *Double Jeopardy and Prosecution Appeals* (Law Com No 267, 2001)

Lord Chancellor's Department, *Government Policy on Archives* (Cm 4516, 1999)

Matthews P, 'The Legal and Moral Limits of Common Law Tracing' in Birks P (ed), *Laundering and Tracing* (Clarendon Press 1995)

Roberts AJ, 'Evidence: Bad Character – Pre-Criminal Justice Act 2003 Law' (2008) 4 Crim LR, 303

NB For more information on using OSCOLA, see Meredith, S. and Nolan, D. (2012) *Oxford University Standard for Citation of Legal Authorities*. 4th edn. Available at: http://www.law.ox.ac.uk/published/OSCOLA_4th_edn_Hart_2012.pdf (Accessed: 14 August 2012).

Section J.
Vancouver referencing style

The Vancouver referencing style is a numeric citation system used in biomedical, health and some science publications. It was first defined in 1978 at the conference of the International Committee of Medical Journal Editors (ICMJE) in Vancouver, Canada, hence its name. It is also known as the Uniform Requirements for Manuscripts Submitted to Biomedical Journals.

Conventions when using the Vancouver referencing style

- Vancouver uses numeric references in the text, either numbers in brackets (1) or **superscript**[1], linked to full **citations** in **footnotes**
- The same citation number is used whenever a source is cited in your text
- These in-text numbers are matched to full, numbered **references** for each publication in a **reference list**
- The reference list lists publications in the order they appeared in the text, not alphabetically
- Very little punctuation is used
- Well-established abbreviations are used for journal titles.

Multiple citations

- If you have written a section of text based upon several references, these are indicated by listing each source separated by a comma.

Example

Several drug trials (3,6,9,12) proved …

Author names

- Authors should be cited by family name, then initials.

Example

James MS

- Note that there is no comma between the family name and initials, nor any full stops after the initials or spaces between the initials. Authors should be listed in the order shown in the article or book, not alphabetically.

Multiple authors

- Many science publications are the result of collaborative work, resulting in multiple authors who require citation. If you have six authors or fewer, list all of them. If there are more than six authors, the ICMJE Uniform Requirements suggests citing the six authors followed by **et al**.

Example

Bourne AD, Davis P, Fuller E, Hanson AJ, Price KN, Vaughan JT, et al.

Organisations as authors

- Names of organisations are spelt out, not abbreviated.

Example

General Medical Council.

No authors identified

- If no authors or editors are listed, use the title of the book, journal article or website.

Editors

- Unlike other citations styles shown in *Cite them right*, the Vancouver system never abbreviates the word 'editor'.

Example

Redclift N, Gibbon S, editors. Genetics: critical concepts in social and cultural theory. London: Routledge; 2007.

Edition

- The abbreviation ed. is used for edition.

Example

Bradley JR, Johnson DR, Pober BR. Medical genetics. 4th ed. Malden, Mass.: Blackwell Science; 2006.

Journal titles

- Journal titles are abbreviated. If the correct abbreviation is not included in the journal article you have used, check the *National Library of Medicine List of Serials Indexed for Online Users* (http://www.nlm.nih.gov/tsd/serials/lsiou.html). Use a capital letter for each word of the abbreviated title, for example Annu Rev Cell Biol is the accepted abbreviation for Annual Review of Cell Biology.

Book titles

- Only the first word and any **proper nouns** or acronyms are capitalised and the title is neither underlined nor italicised.

Example

Cite them right: the essential referencing guide.

Reference list and bibliography

- The reference list should only include sources you have cited in your text. List any sources you read but did not cite in your work in a separate **bibliography**.

How to reference common sources in your reference list

J.1   Books

Citation order:
- Author/editor
- Title (capitalise only the first letter of the first word and any proper nouns)
- Edition (only include the edition number if it is not the first edition)
- Place of publication: publisher;
- Year of publication

Example: single author

Reference list

Ridley M. Genome: the autobiography of a species in 23 chapters. London: Fourth Estate Ltd; 1999.

Example: up to six authors

Reference list

Jones DT, Robson K, Smith TS, Tam KW, Vaughan P, Yates JS. Genetics. 3rd ed. Washington DC: Life Laboratories; 2009.

Example: more than six authors

Reference list

Bourne AD, Davis P, Fuller E, Hanson AJ, Price KN, Vaughan JT, et al. Health systems. London: Fuller Ltd; 2008.

J.2 Ebooks

Citation order:

- Author/editor
- Title of ebook (capitalize only first letter of first word and any proper nouns)
- Edition (only include the edition number if it is not the first edition)
- [ebook]
- Place of publication: publisher;
- Year of original publication
- [cited year month day]
- Available from:
- Title of ebook collection
- URL

Example

Reference list

Templeton AR. Population genetics and microevolutionary theory [Internet]. Hoboken, N.J.: John Wiley and Sons; 2006 [cited 2012 Aug 23]. Available from: http://library.dur.ac.uk/record=b2111435~S1.

J.3 Chapters/sections of edited books

Citation order:

- Author(s) of the chapter/section
- Title of chapter/section
- In
- Name of editor(s) of book
- editor(s)
- Title of book
- Place of publication: publisher;
- Year of publication
- Page numbers (preceded by p.)

Example

Reference list

Hart I. The spread of tumours. In Knowles MA, Selby PJ, editors. Introduction to the cellular and molecular biology of cancer. Oxford: Oxford University Press; 2005. p. 278–88.

J.4 Journal articles

Citation order:

- Author(s)
- Title of article
- Title of journal
- Date of publication as year month day;
- Volume (issue):
- Page numbers (not preceded by p.)

Example

Reference list

Consonni D, De Matteis S, Lubin JH, Wacholder S, Tucker M, Pesatori AC, et al. Lung cancer and occupation in a population-based case-control study. Am J Epidemiol 2010 Feb 1;171(3):323–33.

J.5 Ejournal articles

Citation order:

- Author(s)
- Title of article
- Title of journal (capitalise all initial letters)
- [internet]

- Date of publication as year month day
- [cited year month day];
- Volume (issue):
- Page numbers (not preceded by p.)
- Available from: URL or Digital Object Identifier (doi)

Example: with URL

Reference list

Amr S, Wolpert B, Loffredo CA, Zheng YL, Shields PG, Jones R. Occupation, gender, race and lung cancer. J Occup Environ Med [internet]. 2008 Oct [cited 2012 Aug 23]; 50(10):1167–75. Available from: http://journals.lww.com/joem/Abstract/2008/10000/Occupation,_Gender,_Race,_and_Lung_Cancer.12.aspx

Example: with doi

Reference list

Amr S, Wolpert B, Loffredo CA, Zheng YL, Shields PG, Jones R. Occupation, gender, race and lung cancer. J Occup Environ Med [internet]. 2008 Oct [cited 2012 Aug 23]; 50(10):1167–75. Available from: doi: 10.1097/JOM.0b013e31817d3639

J.6 Electronic articles published ahead of print

Some scientific publishers are making articles available online before they are available in print, after initial review and corrections but before a final version has been submitted by the author. There may be differences between the published ahead-of-print article and the final published version, so you must distinguish in your reference that you are referencing the earlier rather than the final version.

Example

Reference list

Jarvis-Selinger S, Pratt DD, Regehr G. Competency is not enough: integrating identity formation into the medical education discourse. Acad Med [cited 2012 Aug 23]. Epub 2012 Jul 25. Available from: doi: 10.1097/ACM.0b013e3182604968

Note the use of the qualifying phrase 'Epub 2012 Jul 25' in this example, rather than [internet], in the examples of a final published versions above.

J.7 Conference papers

Citation order:
- Author(s)
- Title of conference paper
- Title of conference (capitalise all initial letters, except for linking words)
- Date as year month day(s)
- Location
- If published, add details of place and publisher or journal reference

Example

Reference list

Valberg PA, Watson AY. Lack of concordance between reported lung-cancer risk levels and occupation-specific diesel-exhaust exposure. 3rd Colloquium on Particulate Air Pollution and Human Health; 1999 Jun 6–8; Durham, North Carolina.

J.8 Scientific or technical reports

Citation order:
- Author(s)
- Title of report
- Publishing organisation. Place of publication
- Date of publication
- Report series and number

Example

Reference list

Breslow NE, Day NE. Statistical methods in cancer research. Vol 1. Analysis of case-control studies. International Agency for Research on Cancer, Lyon, France; 1980. IARC Scientific Publication no. 32.

J.9 Research data collections

Citation order:
- Title of data series
- Title of data collection or programme
- Organisation hosting data
- [cited year month day]
- Available from: URL

Example

Reference list

Tumour incidences, Nebraska 1973–83. Surveillance Epidemiology and End Results (SEER) Data 1973–2006. National Cancer Institute (USA). [cited 2012 Aug 23]. Available from: http://seer.cancer.gov/resources/

J.10 Organisation or personal internet sites

Citation order:
- Author
- Title of internet site
- [internet]
- Year that the site was published/last updated
- [cited year month day];
- Number of screens or pages
- Available from: URL

Example

Reference list

Macmillan Cancer Support. Lung cancer. [internet]. 2012 [cited 2012 Aug 23]; [29 screens]. Available from: http://www.macmillan.org.uk/Cancerinformation/Cancertypes/Lung/Lungcancer.aspx

NB For **web pages** where no author can be identified, you should use the title of the web page.

Example

Reference list

WhyQuit.com. [internet] 2012 Aug 13 [cited 2012 Aug 23]; [50+ screens]. Available from: http://whyquit.com/

Sample text

More than 38,000 people are diagnosed with lung cancer every year in the UK. (1) Studies elsewhere have investigated links between occupation or socio-demographic status and cancer (2,3), but smoking is the biggest single cause of lung cancer in the UK. (1) Some researchers have analysed populations to establish incidences of tumours. (4) Tumours may spread from the lungs to elsewhere in the body. (5) Charities and self-help groups provide advice and moral support to victims. (1,6)

Sample reference list

1. Macmillan Cancer Support. Lung cancer. [internet]. 2010 [cited 2012 Aug 23]; [29 screens]. Available from: http://www.macmillan.org.uk/Cancerinformation/Cancertypes/Lung/Lungcancer.aspx

2. Valberg PA, Watson AY. Lack of concordance between reported lung-cancer risk levels and occupation-specific diesel-exhaust exposure. 3rd Colloquium on Particulate Air Pollution and Human Health; 1999 Jun 6–8; Durham, North Carolina.

3. Amr S, Wolpert B, Loffredo CA, Zheng YL, Shields PG, Jones R. Occupation, gender, race and lung cancer. J Occup Environ Med [internet]. 2008 Oct [cited 2012 Aug 23]; 50(10):1167–75. Available from: doi: 10.1097/JOM.0b013e31817d3639

4. Tumour incidences, Nebraska 1973–83. Surveillance Epidemiology and End Results (SEER) Data 1973–2006. National Cancer Institute (USA). [cited 2012 Aug 23]. Available from: http://seer.cancer.gov/resources/

5. Hart I. The spread of tumours. In Knowles MA, Selby PJ, editors. Introduction to the cellular and molecular biology of cancer. Oxford: Oxford University Press; 2005. p. 278–88.

6. WhyQuit.com. [internet] 2012 Aug 13 [cited 2012 Aug 23]; [50+ screens]. Available from: http://whyquit.com/

NB For further information on the Vancouver referencing style, see http://www.nlm.nih.gov/bsd/uniform_requirements.html (accessed: 23 August 2012).

Glossary

Address bar: Also known as location or URL bar, it indicates the current URL, web page address, path to a local file or other item to be located by the browser.

Bibliography: A list of all the sources you consulted for your work arranged in alphabetical order by author's surname or, when there is no author, by title. For web pages where no author or title is apparent, the URL of the web page would be used.

Citation: The in-text reference that gives brief details (for example author, date, page number) of the source you are quoting from or referring to. This citation corresponds with the full details of the work (title, publisher and so on) given in your reference list or bibliography, so that the reader can identify and/or locate the work. End-text citations are more commonly known as references.

Cited Works List: The Modern Language Association's (MLA) equivalent of a reference list that provides full details of the source cited in your text.

Common knowledge: Facts that are generally known.

Digital Object Identifier (doi): A numbered tag used to identify individual digital (online) sources, such as journal articles and conference papers.

Direct quotation: The actual words used by an author, in exactly the same order as in their original work, and with the original spelling. See Section C for more details of how to set out all quotations in your text.

Ellipsis: The omission of words from speech or writing. A set of three dots (…) shows where the original words have been omitted.

End-text citation: An entry in the reference list at the end of your work, which contains the full (bibliographical) details of information for the in-text citation.

***et al.*:** (From the Latin *et alia* meaning 'and others'.) A term most commonly used (for example Harvard author-date system) for works having more than three authors. The citation gives the first surname listed in the publication, followed by *et al*.

Footnote/endnote: An explanatory note and/or source citation either at the foot of the page or end of a chapter used in numeric referencing styles, for example MHRA. These are not used in Harvard and other author-date referencing styles.

***ibid.*:** (From the Latin *ibidem* meaning 'in the same place'.) A term used with citations that refers to an immediately preceding cited work. It is not used in the Harvard system, where works appear only once in the alphabetical list of references.

Internet: The global computer network that provides a variety of information and communication facilities, consisting of interconnected networks using standardised communication protocols.

In-text citation: Often known as simply the citation, this gives brief details (for example author, date, page number) of your source of information within your text.

op. cit.: (From the Latin *opere citato* meaning 'in the work already cited'.) A term used with citations that refers to a previously cited work. It is not used in the Harvard system, where works appear only once in the alphabetical list of references.

Paraphrase: A restating of someone else's thoughts or ideas in your own words. You must always cite your source when paraphrasing (see Section C, p. 9 for more details and an example).

Peer-review: A process used in academic publishing to check the accuracy and quality of a work intended for publication. The author's draft of a book or article is sent by an editor (usually anonymously) to experts in the subject, who suggest amendments or corrections. This process is seen as a guarantee of academic quality and is a major distinction between traditional forms of publishing, such as books and journals, and information in web pages, which can be written by anyone, even if they have no expertise in a subject.

Plagiarism: Taking and using another person's thoughts, writings or inventions as your own without acknowledging or citing the source of the ideas and expressions. In the case of copyrighted material, plagiarism is illegal.

Proper noun: The name of an individual person, place or organisation, having an initial capital letter.

Quotation: The words or sentences from another information source used within your text (see also Direct quotation).

Reference: The full publication details of the work cited.

Reference list: A list of references at the end of your assignment that includes the full information for your citations so that the reader can easily identify and retrieve each work (journal articles, books, web pages and so on).

Secondary referencing: Citing/referencing a work that has been mentioned or quoted in the work you are reading (see Section B, p. 7 for more details and an example).

Short citations: These are used in numeric referencing systems, including MHRA and OSCOLA, instead of *op. cit.* When a work is cited for the first time, all bibliographic details are included in the footnotes/endnotes and in the bibliography reference. If a work is cited more than once in the text, the second and subsequent entries in the footnotes/endnotes use an abbreviated, short citation, such as the author and title (as well as a specific page reference), so that the reader can find the full bibliographic details in the bibliography.

sic: (From the Latin meaning 'so, thus'.) A term used after a quoted or copied word to show that the original word has been written exactly as it appears in the original text, and usually highlights an error or misspelling of the word.

Summarise: Similar to paraphrasing, summarising provides a brief account of someone else's ideas or work, covering only the main points and leaving out the details (see Section C, p. 10 for more details and an example).

Superscript number: A number used in numeric referencing styles (including MHRA and OSCOLA) to identify citations in the text, which is usually smaller than and set above the normal text, that is[1].

URL: The abbreviation for Uniform (or Universal) Resource Locator, the address of documents and other information sources on the internet (for example http://…).

Virtual learning environment (VLE): An online teaching environment (also known as online learning environment – OLE) that allows interaction between tutors and students, and the storage of course documents and teaching materials (see Section E, p. 36 for more details).

Web page: A hypertext document accessible via the World Wide Web (www), the extensive information system on the internet, which provides facilities for documents to be connected to other documents by hypertext links.

Further reading

Avoiding plagiarism

Academy JISC Academic Integrity Service (2010) *Supporting academic integrity: approaches and resources for higher education*. Available at: http://www. heacademy.ac.uk/assets/documents/ academicintegrity/ SupportingAcademicIntegrity_v2.pdf (Accessed: 4 September 2012).

Cardiff University Information Services (no date) *Is it plagiarism quiz*. Available at: https://ilrb. cf.ac.uk/plagiarism/quiz/index.html (Accessed: 4 September 2012).

Carroll, J. (2007) *A handbook for deterring plagiarism in higher education*. 2nd edn. Oxford: Oxford Centre for Staff and Learning Development.

Cottrell, S. (2013) *The study skills handbook*. 4th edn. Basingstoke: Palgrave Macmillan.

Plagiarism: University of Leeds guide. (no date) Available at: http://www.lts.leeds.ac.uk/ plagiarism/ (Accessed: 4 September 2012).

Referencing

American Psychological Association (2009) *Publication manual of the American Psychological Association*, 6th edn (Washington, DC: American Psychological Association).

The Bluebook: a uniform system of citation (2010) Harvard Law Review Association.

British Standards Institution (1990). *BS 5605:1990. Recommendations for citing and referencing published material*. London: BSI.

British Standards Institution (2010). *BS ISO 690. Information and documentation – Guidelines for bibliographic references and citations to information resources.* London: BSI.

The Chicago manual of style. 16th edn. (2010) Chicago: The University of Chicago Press.

House of Commons Information Office (2010) *Factsheet G17: The Official Report*. Available at: http://www.parliament.uk/documents/ upload/g17.pdf (Accessed: 2 September 2012).

Meredith, S. and Nolan, D. (2012) *Oxford University Standard for Citation of Legal Authorities*. 4th edn. Available at: http://www. law.ox.ac.uk/published/OSCOLA_4th_edn_ Hart_2012.pdf (Accessed: 14 August 2012).

Modern Humanities Research Association (2013) *MHRA style guide: a handbook for authors, editors, and writers of theses*. 3rd edn. Available at: http://www.mhra.org.uk/ Publications/Books/StyleGuide/index.html (Accessed: 21 January 2013).

Modern Language Association (2009) *MLA handbook for writers of research papers*. 7th edn. New York: Modern Language Association of America.

U.S. National Library of Medicine (2011) *International Committee of Medical Journal Editors (ICMJE) Uniform requirements for manuscripts submitted to biomedical journals: sample references*. Available at: http://www.nlm.nih.gov/bsd/uniform_ requirements.html (Accessed: 4 September 2012).

Williams, K. and Carroll, J. (2009) *Referencing and understanding plagiarism*. Basingstoke: Palgrave Macmillan.

Index for the Harvard referencing style

NB To avoid confusion when referencing, this index does not list items specific to the alternative referencing styles (Sections F–J)

Index entries are arranged alphabetically letter by letter, with numbers referring to pages

Bold numbers indicate glossary entries